Picture This!

Learning English Through Pictures

D0079875

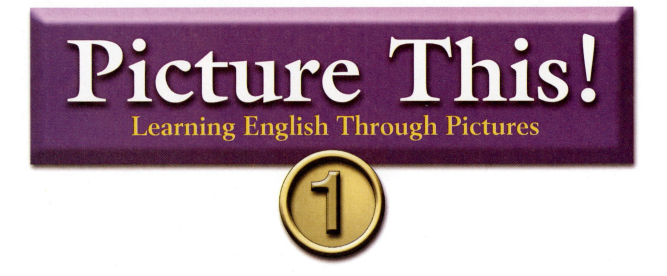

Picture This!
Learning English Through Pictures
1

TIM HARRIS   ALLAN ROWE

PEARSON
Longman

Picture This! Learning English Through Pictures 1

© Copyright 2006 by Pearson Education, Inc.
All rights reserved.
No part of this publication may be reproduced,
stored in a retrieval system, or transmitted
in any form or by any means, electronic, mechanical,
photocopying, recording, or otherwise,
without the prior permission of the publisher.

Pearson Education, 10 Bank Street, White Plains, NY 10606

Cover illustration: Allan Rowe
Text design: Tim Harris
Text composition: Jacqueline Tobin
Text font: 13/15 Times Roman, 13/15 Helvetica
Text art: Allan Rowe
Editor: Suzi Wong

Library of Congress Cataloging-in-Publication Data

Harris, Tim (Timothy A.)
  Picture this! / Tim Harris, Allan Rowe.
      p. cm.
  ISBN 0-13-170336-6 (pbk. : alk. paper)
  1. English language--Textbooks for foreign speakers. 2. English
language--Grammar--Problems, exercises, etc. I. Rowe, Allan. II. Title.
PE1128.H349 2005
428.2'4--dc22
                              2005044852

Printed in the United States of America
1 2 3 4 5 6 7 8 9 10-CRK-10 09 08 07 06 05

To our families

CONTENTS

PREFACE

Picture This! is a two-level multi-skills course for beginning students of English. This innovative course enables students to master the basics, so they can use English effectively for everyday situations.

APPROACH AND METHODOLOGY

The ability of our students to communicate in English involves two tasks at the same time: (1) deciding what they want to say and (2) using the appropriate language to express their thoughts. It's much easier for them to do both things at once if the second task can be done automatically. Our first priority, therefore, is to help students "automatize" basic structures and high-frequency vocabulary, the "core language" they need for communication.

Automatization is the ability of students to remember information and perform tasks without having to stop and think about what they are doing. When information or tasks are automatized, using this information and performing these tasks is almost as effortless as breathing. To help beginning students automatize the core language, *Picture This!* provides intensive practice based on principles of learning that promote memory.

Memory – central to all types of learning – is especially important in language learning because it determines how well students are able to use the language after they leave the classroom. If we understand how memory can be made stronger – for example, by visualization, by rehearsal, by transformation, or by writing – we can design lessons that will help our students improve their memory for the material they must learn. To enhance memory, *Picture This!* uses a range of picture-based lessons in an integrated skills approach to learning.

PICTURE-BASED LESSONS: It is all too easy for students to forget language or concepts that are "explained" in class. It is much easier to remember concepts that are shown or demonstrated, and pictures, by their very nature, show instead of tell. The lively and engaging illustrations in *Picture This!* make it easy for students to learn and remember the words for people, places, objects, and characteristics. The artwork also provides effective and meaningful practice with basic structures and language functions. Learning experts tell us an excellent way to remember something is to change it, to transform it in some way. To help students remember new grammar and vocabulary, *Picture This!* asks students to express in words the instructional information contained in the pictures. By taking something *visual* and making it *verbal*, the students are transforming information and filing it in their active working memory.

INTEGRATED SKILLS: In *Picture This!* the four skills of language learning (listening, speaking, reading, and writing) are usually combined in the same lesson. A typical lesson contains several pictures demonstrating a particular grammatical structure or language function. The students hear the target structure as they listen to conversations about the pictures, and they repeat the questions and answers they hear on the recordings. The students are encouraged to recreate the conversations with information provided by the pictures. They also write the sentences containing the target structure, which they then read aloud. By the end of the lesson, all four skills have been applied to learning a single structure, and when this happens, student retention increases dramatically.

Picture This! offers a true integrated skills approach to learning, with lessons designed in such a way that one skill improves another. Particular attention is given to integrating the writing skill, as writing can do so much to foster acquisition of the other skills. For example, it's a great advantage when students get in the habit of writing down their "talk" because this makes their thinking – and their mistakes – visible. So we suggest having students go to the board and write the language forms they have been practicing orally. With a little assistance, students are able to correct their own mistakes in grammar and spelling. This opportunity enables students to take risks, to monitor their progress, and to improve their ability to communicate – both orally and in writing.

LEARNING ENGLISH THROUGH PICTURES: The detailed illustrations in *Picture This!* make key vocabulary easily comprehensible to students, so they can perform a range of meaningful tasks from the first day of class. Packed with visual information, the illustrations provide frequent opportunities to go beyond the lesson on the page and engage in more spontaneous, less-structured activities. The illustrations present a cast of colorful characters in all kinds of situations, often humorous, for students to talk about. Having conversations about fictional characters paves the way for students to talk about their own life experiences. The warm, evocative illustrations in *Picture This!* make learning English more personal and enjoyable for the students.

WHAT EACH CHAPTER CONTAINS

Cartoon Story   The grammar of each chapter is introduced in an entertaining cartoon story that demonstrates the use of natural speech and conversational expressions. The stories personalize the themes and functions covered in the curriculum.

Grammar   Picture-based lessons provide thorough, systematic, and meaningful practice with the grammatical structures introduced in each chapter.

Listening   The listening activities are integrated with oral activities and writing exercises to develop students' ability to understand, reproduce, and remember what they hear.

Speaking   Students develop their speaking ability through a variety of activities including guided conversations, role plays, and free response questions that allow students to talk about themselves. Imaginative illustrations suggest many opportunities for creative language practice.

Reading   Various types of texts enable students to steadily develop their reading skills as they learn new grammar and vocabulary. Stimulating topics create motivated readers and opportunities for discussion.

Writing   The writing exercises reinforce core language and help students develop their listening, speaking, and reading skills.

Pronunciation   Each chapter includes a section with exercises that focus on pronunciation points, such as vowel and consonant sounds, plurals, stress and intonation.

Life Skills   Everyday life situations provide contexts for learning basic competencies in the areas that are most important to students: food, clothing, transportation, work, housing, and health care.

COURSE COMPONENTS:

The text of *Picture This!* is recorded on three CDs. An interleaved Teacher's Edition provides practical teaching tips, expansion activities, and answer keys.

CONTENTS

Chapter 1

MEETING AND GREETING PEOPLE

▶ **CONVERSATION 1**
🎧 *Listen. Listen and practice.*

▶ **PAIR WORK 1** • *Introduce yourself to other students.*

A: Hello. My name is _____.

B: I'm _____.

A: Nice to meet you, _____.

B: Nice to meet you, too.

▶ **CONVERSATION 2**
🎧 *Listen. Listen and practice.*

MARIA: Hi. How are you?

CARLOS: I'm fine. And you?

MARIA: Fine, thank you.

▶ **PAIR WORK 2** • *Have similar conversations.*

INTRODUCING SOMEONE

▶ **CONVERSATION 1**

🎧 *Listen. Listen and practice.*

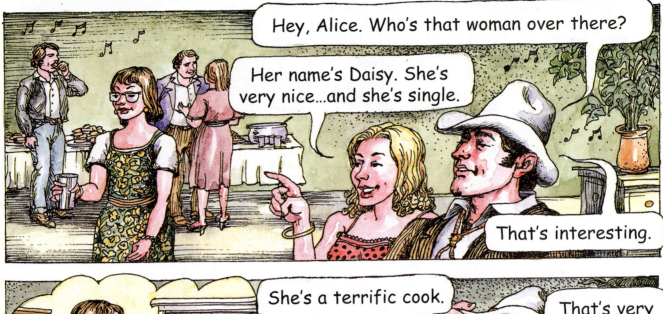

▶ **CONVERSATION 2**

🎧 *Listen. Listen and practice.*

DAISY: Hi, Alice. Who's your friend?

ALICE: Daisy, this is Dallas.

DAISY: Nice to meet you.

DALLAS: Nice to meet you, too.

▶ **GROUP WORK** • *Have similar conversations with two other students. Use your own names.*

OCCUPATIONS

▶ 🎧 *Look and listen. Listen and repeat.*

1. This is John Denby.
   He's a teacher.

2. This is Susan Chen.
   She's a doctor.

3. This is Carlos Bravo.
   He's a mechanic.

4. This is Daisy Miller.
   She's a chef.

5. This is Mike Kelly.
   He's a pilot.

6. This is Betty Jones.
   She's a banker.

7. This is Peter Gamble.
   He's a businessman.

8. This is Maria Lopez.
   She's a carpenter.

9. This is Grover Muldoon.
   He's a police officer.

Is	he she	a pilot? a doctor?		Yes,	he she	is.		No,	he she	isn't.

🎧 *Listen. Listen and repeat.*

PAIR WORK • *Practice the conversations.*

WRITING • *Fill in the answers. Then read the conversations aloud.*

LOCATIONS

Where	's (is)	Jimmy? Alice?

He She	's (is)	at the park. at the office.

 *Listen. Listen and practice.*

Is	Jimmy Alice	at the park? at work?		Yes,	he she	is.		No,	he she	isn't.

🎧 *Listen. Listen and repeat.*

PAIR WORK • *Practice the conversations.*

WRITING • *Fill in the answers. Then read the conversations aloud.*

NUMBERS

▶ 🎧 *Listen and repeat.*

0	1	2	3	4	5	6	7	8	9	10
zero (oh)	one	two	three	four	five	six	seven	eight	nine	ten

▶ **CONVERSATION**
🎧 *Listen.*

What's your name?

Ken Honda.

PUBLIC LIBRARY

▶ **WRITING** • *Write your name, address and phone number.*

LIBRARY CARD

Name: _Ken Honda_

Address: _529 Maple Street_

Portland, Oregon

Phone Number: _(503) 825-3906_

LIBRARY CARD

Name:_____

Address:_____

_____

Phone Number:_____

▶ **PAIR WORK** • *Ask the person next to you:*

• What's your name?
• What's your address?
• What's your phone number?

TIME

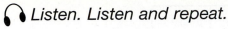 Listen. Listen and repeat.

What time is it?
It's seven o'clock.

What time is it?
It's twelve o'clock.

What time is it?
It's four o'clock.

▶ **PAIR WORK** • *Ask and answer questions.*

A: **What time is it?**
B: **It's eleven o'clock.**

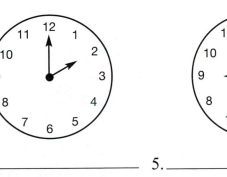

1. _It's eleven o'clock._   2. _____   3. _____

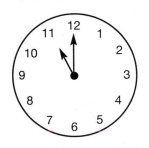

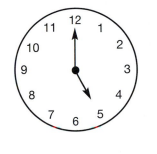

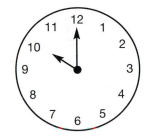

4. _____   5. _____   6. _____

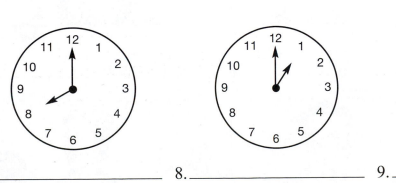

7. _____   8. _____   9. _____

▶ **WRITING** • *Write the time under each clock.*

GRAMMAR • This/That

What	's (is)	this? that?		It	's (is)	a cat. a dog.

▶ 🎧 *This is an English class for international students. Listen. Listen and practice.*

Is	this that	a table? a chair?	Yes, it is.	No, it isn't.

🎧 *Listen. Listen and repeat.*

▶ **PAIR WORK** • *Practice the conversations.*

GRAMMAR • These/Those

What	are	these? those?

They	're (are)	apples. pears.

▶ 🎧 *Listen. Listen and practice.*

| Are | these those | flowers? trees? | | Yes, they are. | | No, they aren't. |

▶ 🎧 *Listen. Listen and repeat.*   ▶ **PAIR WORK** • *Practice the conversations.*

1. Are these glasses? — No, they aren't. They're cups.

2. Are those bananas? — Yes, they are.

3. Are those bottles?

4. Are these flowers?

5. Are these pears?

6. Are those bananas?

7. Are those trees?

8. Are these magazines?

▶ **WRITING** • *Fill in the answers. Then read the conversations aloud.*

GRAMMAR • Prepositions

▶ 🎧 *Look and listen. Listen and repeat.*

The bird is **in** the cage.

The cat is **under** the cage.

The cat is **on** the table.

The cat is **next to** the cage.

The bird is **in front of** the cat.

The man is **behind** the cat.

▶ **PAIR WORK** • *Ask and answer questions. Choose the correct preposition.*

Example: **Where are the birds?**
They're in the tree.

1. Where's Billy?
   He's (under/on) the tree.

2. Where's the ball?
   It's (behind/in front of) Billy.

3. Where's the bicycle?
   It's (next to/in) the tree.

4. Where's the dog?
   It's (in front of/behind) the tree.

5. Where are the apples?
   They're (in/under) the basket.

6. Where's the basket?
   It's (next to/on) the table.

▶ **WRITING** • *Complete the sentences using these prepositions:*
in, on, under, next to, behind, in front of.

Example: The wastebasket is __in front of__ the desk.

1. Mr. Denby is _____ the desk.

2. Becky is _____ Mr. Denby.

3. The books are _____ the desk.

4. The flowers are _____ the vase.

5. The vase is _____ the books.

6. The cat is _____ the door.

7. The chair is _____ the desk.

8. The coat is _____ the chair.

9. The umbrella is _____ the chair.

10. The paper cups are _____ the wastebasket.

▶ **PAIR WORK** • *Ask and answer questions.*

paper cups

A: **Where are the paper cups?**
B: **They're in the wastebasket.**

wastebasket

A: **Where is the wastebasket?**
B: **It's in front of the desk.**

1. cat
2. books
3. umbrella
4. Mr. Denby
5. Becky
6. flowers
7. coat
8. chair
9. paper cups

Where are you from?

CONVERSATION 1

🎧 *Listen. Listen and practice.*

PIERRE: Hello. My name is Pierre.

HIROKO: Hi, I'm Hiroko.

PIERRE: Where are you from?

HIROKO: Japan. And you?

PIERRE: I'm from France.

PAIR WORK • *Have similar conversations. Use your own information.*

A: Hello. My name is _____.

B: Hi. I'm _____.

A: Where are you from?

B: _____. And you?

A: I'm from _____.

CONVERSATION 2

🎧 *Listen. Listen and practice.*

MARINA: Who's that?

HIROKO: His name's Pierre.

MARINA: Where's he from?

HIROKO: He's from France.

CONVERSATION 3

🎧 *Listen. Listen and practice.*

OMAR: Who's that?

LUIS: Her name's Hiroko.

OMAR: Where's she from?

LUIS: She's from Japan.

▶ **PAIR WORK** • *Have similar conversations about other students in your class.*

GRAMMAR • Wh- Questions

▶ **WRITING** • *Write a question for each answer. Then read the conversations aloud.*

VOCABULARY

NOUNS

Occupations	Places	Other		
banker	bank	apple	chair	man
businessman	beach	ball	coat	newspaper
carpenter	garage	banana	cup	pear
chef	hospital	basket	desk	table
doctor	library	bicycle	dog	tree
firefighter	office	bird	door	umbrella
mechanic	park	book	flower	vase
pilot	post office	bottle	friend	wastebasket
police officer	supermarket	cage	glass	woman
teacher		cat	magazine	

SUBJECT PRONOUNS
I
you
he
she
it
they

POSSESSIVE ADJECTIVES
my
your
his
her

PREPOSITIONS
in
on
under
next to
in front of
behind

VERB
be

ADVERB
(over) there

ADJECTIVES
interesting
terrific

ARTICLES
a/an
the

WH-WORDS
who
what
where

CONJUNCTION
and

INTERJECTION
Hey.

EXPRESSIONS

Greeting people
Hi. How are you?
   I'm fine. And you?
Fine, thank you.

Introducing yourself
Hello. My name is…
   I'm…
Nice to meet you.
   Nice to meet you, too.

Introducing someone
…, this is…
   Hi. It's nice to meet you.

Asking about people
Who's that?
   His/Her name's…
Where's he/she from?
   He/She's from…

Exchanging personal information
What's your name?
   I'm…/My name's…
What's your phone number?
   It's…
What's your address?
   It's…

Asking for the time
What time is it?
   It's two o'clock.

Other
She's single.
That's interesting.

STRESS

▶ **A** 🎧 *Listen to the stressed vowels. Listen and repeat.*

dóctor	ba**ná**na	gui**tár**
stúdent	A**mé**rica	hel**ló**
líbrary	lo**cá**tion	intro**dúce**
ínteresting	ter**rí**fic	com**pléte**

▶ **B** 🎧 *Listen and mark the stressed vowels. Then read these words out loud.*

example	garage	bicycle
number	mechanic	police
Japan	address	hospital
umbrella	behind	conversation

▶ **C** 🎧 *Listen. Notice the main stress in these sentences. Listen and practice.*

A: **Héy**, **Á**lice. **Whó's** that **wó**man over **thére**?

B: Her **náme** is **Dá**isy. She's very **níce**…and she's **sín**gle.

A: **Thát's** interesting.

B: She's a ter**rí**fic **cóok**.

A: That's **vé**ry interesting.

▶ **D** 🎧 *Listen and mark the main stress in these sentences. Then practice the conversation with a partner.*

A: Hello. My name is Omar.

B: Hi. I'm Hiroko.

A: Where are you from?

B: Japan. And you?

A: I'm from Somalia.

GRAMMAR SUMMARY

TO BE Affirmative

He She It	's (is)	
I	'm (am)	in the library.
You We They	're (are)	

Negative

He She It	isn't (is not) 's not	
I	'm not (am not)	in the library.
You We They	aren't (are not) 're not	

Interrogative

Is	he she it	
Am	I	in the library?
Are	you we they	

Short Answers

Yes,	he she it	is.		No,	he she it	isn't.
	I	am.			I	'm not.
	you we they	are.			you we they	aren't.

Question with WHAT

What	's (is)	this? that?
	are	these? those?

SINGULAR AND PLURAL NOUNS

It	's (is)	a chair. a table.
They	're (are)	flowers. trees.

Question with WHERE

Where	's (is)	Mr. Gamble?
	's (is)	the newspaper?
	are	the books?

PREPOSITIONS

He	's (is)	at in	the post office.
It	's (is)	on under next to behind in front of	the table.
They	are		

CONTENTS

Chapter

▶ 🎧 *Listen. Listen and practice.*

▶ **PAIR WORK** • *Ask each other the same questions.*

A: **Are you hungry?**

B: **Yes, I am.** OR **No, I'm not.**

▶ 🎧 *Look and listen. Listen and repeat.*

① She's happy.

② He's nervous.

③ She's married.

④ He's rich.

⑤ He's a good singer.

⑥ He's a bad dancer.

⑦ She's a good cook.

⑧ She's a bad driver.

⑨ She's interested in the news.

⑩ He's interested in sports.

⑪ She's afraid of dogs.

⑫ He's afraid of spiders.

▶ **PAIR WORK** • *Ask each other questions.*

A: **Are you hungry?**

B: **Yes, I am.** OR **No, I'm not.**

1. Are you happy?
2. Are you nervous?
3. Are you married?
4. Are you rich?
5. Are you a good singer?
6. Are you a good dancer?
7. Are you a good cook?
8. Are you a good driver?
9. Are you interested in the news?
10. Are you interested in sports?
11. Are you afraid of dogs?
12. Are you afraid of spiders?

GRAMMAR • Adjectives

Joe	is	married.	He's	a married man.
The car		new.	It's	a new car.

▶ 🎧 *Look and listen. Listen and repeat.*

1. Joe is married.   Carlos is single.

2. Sara is happy.   Linda is sad.

3. Mary is rich.   Jane is poor.

4. Ben is strong.   Fred is weak.

5. Snow White is beautiful.   The witch is ugly.

6. Peter is handsome.   The Wolfman is ugly.

7. Nick is hot.   Max is cold.

8. The car is new.   The truck is old.

▶ **WRITING** • *Fill in the answers. Then read the conversations aloud.*

GRAMMAR • Adjectives

The students The apples	are	young. big.	They're	young students. big apples.

▶ 🎧 *Look and listen. Listen and repeat.*

1. They're young.   They're old.

2. They're noisy.   They're quiet.

3. They're fat.   They're thin.

4. They're tall.   They're short.

5. The boots are old.   The shoes are new.

6. The glasses are clean.   The dishes are dirty.

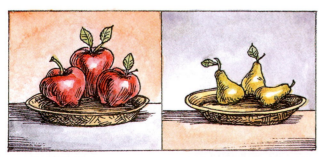

7. The apples are big.   The pears are small.

8. The bananas are cheap.   The oranges are expensive.

▶ **WRITING** • *Fill in the answers. Then read the conversations aloud.*

NUMBERS and TELLING TIME

▶ 🎧 **NUMBERS** • *Listen and repeat.*

11 eleven	**21** twenty-one	**40** forty
12 twelve	**22** twenty-two	**50** fifty
13 thirteen	**23** twenty-three	**60** sixty
14 fourteen	**24** twenty-four	**70** seventy
15 fifteen	**25** twenty-five	**80** eighty
16 sixteen	**26** twenty-six	**90** ninety
17 seventeen	**27** twenty-seven	**100** one hundred
18 eighteen	**28** twenty-eight	**105** one hundred five
19 nineteen	**29** twenty-nine	**110** one hundred ten
20 twenty	**30** thirty	**125** one hundred twenty-five

▶ 🎧 **TELLING TIME** • *Listen and repeat.*

It's two o'clock.

It's two-oh-five.
It's five after two.

It's two fifteen.
It's a quarter past two.

It's two-thirty.
It's half past two.

It's two forty-five.
It's a quarter to three.

It's two fifty-five.
It's five to three.

TIME

▶ **PAIR WORK** • *Ask and answer questions.*

   A: **What time is it?**
   B: **It's nine-twenty.** OR **It's twenty after nine.**

1 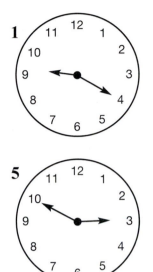   **2** 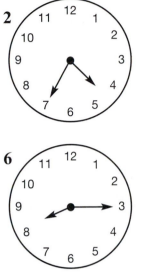   **3** 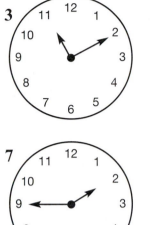   **4**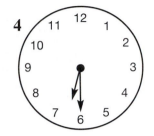

5   **6**   **7**   **8**

▶ 🎧 **TIMES OF DAY** • *Look, listen and read.*

It's seven o'clock **in the morning**.
It's time for breakfast.

It's one o'clock **in the afternoon**.
It's lunchtime.

It's seven o'clock **in the evening**.
It's dinnertime.

It's ten o'clock **at night**.
It's bedtime.

NOUNS

SINGULAR NOUNS • *Complete the sentences with **a** or **an**.*

• Use **a** before a consonant sound: b c k f l m p r
• Use **an** before a vowel sound: a e i o u

1. It's __an__ apple.

2. It's __a__ peach.

3. It's _____ orange.

4. It's _____ pencil.

5. It's _____ eraser.

6. It's _____ watch.

7. It's _____ umbrella.

8. It's _____ letter.

9. It's _____ dictionary.

PLURAL NOUNS • *Change the nouns from singular to plural.*

• Add **s** to make a plural noun: students, books, chairs
• Add **es** to words that end in -s, -ch, -sh: glasses, dishes
• Change **y** to **i** and add **es**: cities
• Irregular: man – men   woman – women   child – children

1. man __men__

2. car __cars__

3. watch _____

4. flower _____

5. tree _____

6. woman _____

7. dictionary _____

8. umbrella _____

9. peach _____

10. family _____

11. student _____

12. class _____

Family

COLORS · CLOTHES

▶ 🎧 *Look and listen. Listen and repeat.*

● red ● orange ● yellow ● green ● blue ○ white ● black ● gray ● brown ● beige

1. dress — shoes
2. jacket — belt — pants
3. blouse — skirt
4. hat — tie — coat
5. shirt — blue jeans — boots
6. shorts — socks — sweater

▶ **PRACTICE** · *What color are their clothes?*

1. Her dress is red. Her shoes are black.

▶ 🎧 *Listen. Listen and practice.*

1. Those are good-looking boots.
   Thank you.

2. And that's a beautiful hat!
   Thanks.

▶ **PAIR WORK** · *Give the people near you a compliment.*

LIFE SKILL • Shopping

▶ 🎧 **DICTATION** • *Listen to the conversations. Listen and fill in the answers.*

1. **How much is this sweater?**
   Eighty-five dollars.

2. **How much are those jeans?**

3. **How much are these socks?**

4. **How much is that handbag?**

5. **How much is this belt?**

6. **How much are those gloves?**

▶ **PAIR WORK** • *Practice the conversations.*

▶ 🎧 **DICTATION** • *Listen to the conversations. Listen and fill in the questions.*

this   that   these   those   dress   jacket   pants   shirt   shoes   sunglasses

How much are these sunglasses?

Sixty-nine dollars.

1.

One hundred fifty dollars.

2.

Ninety-eight dollars.

3.

One hundred and ten dollars.

4.

Seventy-five dollars.

5.

Thirty-nine dollars.

6.

▶ **PAIR WORK** • *Practice the conversations.*

GRAMMAR • Commands

▶ 🎧 *Look and listen. Listen and repeat.*

Note: Use *please* to be more polite. ⟶ Please wait for me.

Please answer the phone!

PRACTICE • *Read the commands out loud.*

▶ 🎧 *Look and listen. Listen and repeat.*

▶ **PRACTICE** • *Read the commands out loud.*

▶ **PRACTICE** • *Read the commands out loud.*

VOCABULARY

NOUNS

Clothes
belt
blouse
boots
coat
dress
gloves
hat
jacket
jeans
pants
shirt
shoes
shorts
skirt
socks
sweater
tie

Colors
beige
black
blue
brown
gray
green
orange
red
white
yellow

Meals
breakfast
lunch
dinner

Other
avocados
basketball player
brother
bus
cake
carrots
class
cookies
dancer
daughter
dictionary
dishes
driver
eraser
hand
keys
kitchen
letter
man
money
mouth
neighbor
oranges
peaches
pencil
singer
sofa
spinach
student
sunglasses
watch
window

VERBS
answer
buy
come
eat
forget
listen to
look at
open
play
relax
sit down
sleep
take
talk
wait for
wash
wear

ADJECTIVES

happy ≠ sad
rich ≠ poor
strong ≠ weak
big ≠ small
tall ≠ short
fat ≠ thin
young ≠ old
married ≠ single

hot ≠ cold
new ≠ old
clean ≠ dirty
noisy ≠ quiet
cheap ≠ expensive
beautiful ≠ ugly
handsome ≠ ugly
good-looking ≠ ugly

good
bad
hungry
thirsty
tired
afraid
nervous
comfortable

ADVERBS

Time Expressions
in the morning
in the afternoon
in the evening
at night

EXPRESSIONS

Telling the time
It's five after two.
It's two-fifteen.
It's a quarter past two.
It's two-thirty.
It's a quarter to three.
It's five to three.

Using time expressions
It's lunchtime.
It's dinnertime.
It's bedtime.

Giving a compliment
That's a beautiful hat.
Those are good-looking boots.

Describing clothing
Her dress is red.
His pants are brown.

Other
He's interested in…
She's afraid of…

PRONUNCIATION

▶ **A** 🎧 Listen to these plural nouns. Notice the pronunciation of the **s** endings.

/s/	/z/	/iz/
books	keys	dishes
students	doors	glasses
desks	windows	peaches

▶ **B** 🎧 Listen and repeat.

▶ **C** 🎧 Listen to the plural forms of these nouns. Listen and repeat.

1. rose

2. dog

3. cat

4. dish

5. bird

6. watch

7. truck

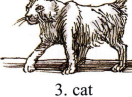

8. camera

9. map

10. radio

11. glass

12. stamp

▶ **D** Complete the chart with the plural forms of the nouns in Part C.

/s/	/z/	/iz/
cats		

▶ **E** 🎧 Listen and check your answers.

GRAMMAR SUMMARY

ADJECTIVES AND WORD ORDER

The bicycle is new. The flowers are beautiful.	It's a new bicycle. They're beautiful flowers.

IMPERATIVE

Close the door!
Open the window!

NEGATIVE IMPERATIVE

Don't	close the door! open the window!

INDEFINITE ARTICLE

It's	a	pear. banana.		It's	an	apple. orange.

Question with HOW MUCH

How much	is the watch? are the books?		It's ninety-five dollars. They're twenty dollars.

CONTENTS

Chapter 3

CARTOON STORY

▶ 🎧 *Dallas is calling his new girlfriend, Daisy. Listen. Listen and practice.*

► QUESTIONS

1. Where is Dallas?
2. Who's he calling?
3. Is Daisy busy now?
4. What's she doing?
5. Is Dallas coming to see Daisy?
6. What's he bringing?
7. Is Daisy happy? Why?

GRAMMAR • Present Continuous

▶ 🎧 *Listen. Listen and practice.*

▶ 🎧 *Listen to the conversations.*

▶ **WRITING** • *Write a question for each picture using the questions in the box.*

Are you thinking about the weekend? Are you enjoying this class? Are you listening to me?
Are you learning a lot in school? Are you wearing new shoes? Are you eating something?

PAIR WORK • *Ask each other the same questions.*

A: **Are you learning a lot in school?**

B: **Yes, I am. My classes are very interesting. OR No, I'm not. My classes are boring.**

GRAMMAR • Present Continuous

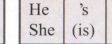

| What | 's (is) | he she | doing? | He She | 's (is) | listening to the radio. |

▶ 🎧 *Listen. Listen and repeat.*

▶ **PAIR WORK** • *Practice the conversations.*

▶ **WRITING** • *Fill in the answers. Then read the conversations aloud.*

Who's Maria dancing with?

She's dancing with Carlos.

1.

Where's Billy going?

2.

What's Daisy reading?

3.

Who's Becky talking to?

4.

GRAMMAR • Present Continuous

Affirmative		
He She	's (is)	listening to the radio.

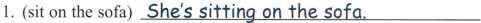

Negative		
He She	isn't (is not)	watching TV.

▶ **WRITING** • *Write affirmative and negative sentences about the people in the pictures. After you finish, read the sentences out loud.*

1. (sit on the sofa) <u>She's sitting on the sofa.</u>
2. (watch television) <u>She isn't watching television.</u>
3. (talk on the phone) _____
4. (read the newspaper) _____

5. (listen to the radio) _____
6. (play the guitar) _____
7. (stand) _____
8. (sit) _____

9. (read a book) _____
10. (write a letter) _____
11. (drink coffee) _____
12. (eat candy) _____

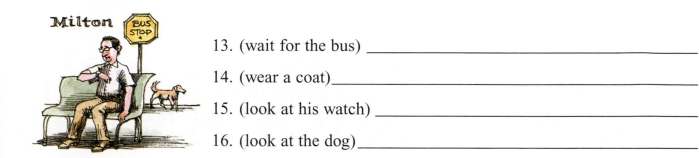

13. (wait for the bus) _____
14. (wear a coat) _____
15. (look at his watch) _____
16. (look at the dog) _____

GRAMMAR • Present Continuous

Yes/No Question		
Is	he she	working?

Short Answers					
Yes,	he she	is.	No,	he she	isn't.

▶ **PAIR WORK** • *Ask and answer questions.*

1. A: **Is Mario singing?**
   B: **Yes, he is.**

2. A: **Is Jane buying a television?**
   B: **No, she isn't. She's buying a computer.**

3. Is Jimmy playing basketball?

4. Is Ken studying at home?

5. Is Daisy going to the market?

6. Is Milton waiting for the bus?

7. Is Becky standing by the window?

8. Is Carlos playing the piano?

9. Is Maria wearing a green dress?

GRAMMAR • Present Continuous

What are they doing?	They	're (are)	making dinner.

▸ 🎧 *Listen. Listen and repeat.*

▸ **PAIR WORK** • *Practice the conversations.*

▸ **WRITING** • *Fill in the answers. Then read the conversations aloud.*

Who are the neighbors talking to?

They're talking to a police officer.

1.

Where are Ken and Suzi having lunch?

2.

What are the men drinking?

3.

Who are the students waiting for?

4.

Where are your friends going?

5.

What are Jimmy and Becky eating?

6.

Who are the people looking at?

7.

Where are Lucy and Grover shopping?

8.

What are they buying?

9.

GRAMMAR • Present Continuous

Affirmative		
They	're (are)	listening to music.

Negative		
They	aren't (are not)	watching TV.

▶ **CLASS ACTIVITY** • *Look at the picture of Grover and Lucy. Where are they? What are they doing? Are they happy? Are they having a good time?*

▶ **WRITING** • *Write affirmative and negative sentences about Grover and Lucy. After you finish, read the sentences out loud.*

1. (sit in front of the fire) <u>They're sitting in front of the fire.</u>

2. (stand by the window) <u>They aren't standing by the window.</u>

3. (drink coffee) _____

4. (listen to music) _____

5. (watch television) _____

6. (play the piano) _____

7. (smile) _____

8. (have a good time) _____

9. (look at the clock) _____

10. (read the newspaper) _____

GRAMMAR • Present Continuous

Yes/No Question	Short Answers	
Are they working?	Yes, they are.	No, they aren't.

▶ **PAIR WORK** • *Ask and answer questions.*

1. A: **Are the girls walking to school?**
   B: **No, they aren't. They're taking the bus.**

2. A: **Are the men singing?**
   B: **Yes, they are.**

3. Are Mr. and Mrs. Lee listening to the radio?

4. Are Lucy and Grover making dinner?

5. Are the boys studying?

6. Are Jack and Jill talking on the phone?

7. Are Maria and Carlos singing?

8. Are the children smiling?

9. Are Becky and Jimmy listening to the teacher?

| Look at | Mike.
Diana.
Jack and Jill.
Lisa and me.
the clock. | Look at | him.
her.
them.
us.
it. |

🎧 *Look and listen. Listen and repeat.*

1. Look at him. He's really strong.

2. She's a good dancer. Look at her.

3. Look at me. I'm beautiful.

4. We're clowns. Look at us.

5. Look at them. They're acrobats.

6. This is a real diamond. Look at it.

GRAMMAR • Object Pronouns

▶ 🎧 Listen.   ▶ **WRITING** • *Fill in the blanks with* **her, him, me, us, it, them**.

1. Call the waiter. Ask <u>him</u> for the menu.

2. Waiter! Please bring ____ the menu.

3. How's your dinner? Are you enjoying ____?

4. Here's my phone number. Call ____ next week.

5. Those glasses are ugly. Don't buy _____.

6. Fern's a good student. Ask _____ for help.

LIBRARY

7. We're leaving now. Please wait for _____.

8. Where's the newspaper? You're sitting on ____.

9. I'm hungry. Bring ____ something to eat.

10. Look! There's Annie! That's ____ over there.

11. Those are my apples! Don't eat _____!

12. Don't be afraid of ____. He's very friendly.

WEATHER

▶ 🎧 *Listen. Listen and practice.*

▶ **PAIR WORK** • *Talk about the weather in each city.*

1. Rio de Janeiro

   A: **How's the weather in Rio de Janeiro?**

   B: **It's sunny and hot.**

SEASONS

▶ 🎧 *Listen.*

Mary is showing some family photos to her friend, Alice. Listen to what Mary says about each photo. Then read her comments out loud.

It's **winter**. We're in the mountains. It's snowing, and it's very cold. But we're having fun. We're making a big snow man.

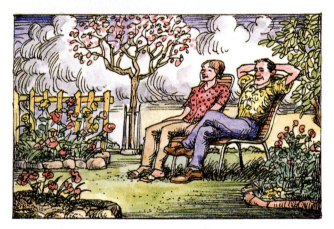

It's **spring**. We're enjoying the pretty flowers in our backyard. It's a cloudy day, but the weather is nice and warm.

It's **summer**. We're spending a day at the beach. The weather is sunny and hot. We're drinking ice-cold lemonade.

It's **fall**. We're taking a walk in the park. The weather is windy and cool, and the leaves are falling. It's a beautiful day.

▶ **QUESTIONS**
- How's the weather in your city today?
- What season is it now?
- What's your favorite season?
- What's your favorite place in the summer?

VOCABULARY

NOUNS

Seasons of the year

winter
spring
summer
fall

Other

acrobat
backyard
barbershop
bird
boyfriend
candy
cell phone
clown
cowboy
diamond
downtown
fire
friend
glasses
guitar
help
lemonade
menu
mountains
people
phone
photo
radio
spaghetti
television
waiter
weekend

VERBS

bring
call
dance
drink
drive
enjoy
fall
learn
look
shop
sing
smile
spend
stand
study
take
think (about)
walk
work

PRONOUNS

Object pronouns

you
me
him
her
us
them
it

Other

something

ADJECTIVES

boring
dumb
favorite
friendly
ice-cold

EXPRESSIONS

Talking about the weather

How's the weather?
   It's hot/warm/cool/cold.
   It's sunny/cloudy/windy.
   It's raining/snowing.

Talking on the phone

Hello there.
   Who's calling? Is that you, _____ ?
Yes, it's me. Are you busy?
   Not really.

Saying goodbye

Bye, bye.
See you soon.

Giving a compliment

You look so handsome.

Showing appreciation

That's very sweet of you.

Other

We're taking a walk.
We're having a good time.

I'm okay.
I'm on my way.

I'm driving in heavy traffic.
That's terrible.

Right now.
Aw, shucks.

INTONATION

▶ 🎧 *Listen. Notice the rising and falling intonation of the questions. Listen and practice.*

CONVERSATION 1

A: Where's Suzi? ↘

B: She's at the library.

A: Is she studying? ↗

B: Yes, she is.

CONVERSATION 2

A: Is David working at the office? ↗

B: No, he isn't. He's at home.

A: What's he doing? ↘

B: He's playing the piano.

NOTE:	Yes/No questions have a rising intonation at the end. Wh- questions have a falling intonation at the end.

▶ 🎧 *Listen and write ↗ for the rising intonation and ↘ for the falling intonation at the end of the questions. After you finish, practice the conversation with a partner.*

A: Hello, there.

B: Dallas, is that you?

A: Yes, it's me. I'm calling you on my cell phone.

B: Where are you?

A: I'm nearby. Are you busy?

B: Not really.

A: What are you doing?

B: I'm making lunch. Are you coming to see me?

A: Yes…here I am!

GRAMMAR SUMMARY

PRESENT CONTINUOUS Affirmative

He She	's (is)	
I	'm (am)	working today.
You We They	're (are)	

Negative

He She	isn't (is not) 's not	
I	'm not (am not)	working today.
You We They	aren't (are not) 're not	

Interrogative

Is	he she	
Am	I	working today?
Are	you we they	

Short Answers

Yes,	he she	is.	No,	he she	isn't.
	I	am.		I	'm not.
	you we they	are.		you we they	aren't.

Questions with WHO, WHAT, WHERE

Who What Where	's (is)	Jill talking to? Jack looking at? Mr. Davis going?	Her friend. The clock. To the library.

OBJECT PRONOUNS

Look at	Mike. Diana. Jack and Jill. Lisa and me. the clock.	Look at	him. her. them. us. it.

CONTENTS

Chapter

4

CARTOON STORY

▶ 🎧 *Listen. Listen and practice.*

STORY QUESTIONS

1. Where is the Rainbow Dance Studio?
2. Who is Jason's dance teacher?
3. Is she very friendly?
4. Why is Jason nervous?
5. What dance is Jason learning?
6. Is it easy or difficult?
7. Is Jason a good student?
8. Is he having a good time?

GRAMMAR REVIEW • Present Continuous

▶ 🎧 *Listen.*　　▶ **WRITING** • *Where are these people? What are they doing?*

1. Mike <u>is at the hospital.</u>

   <u>He's visiting his aunt.</u>

2. Lois and her kids <u>are at the zoo.</u>

   <u>They're looking at a gorilla.</u>

3. Jane _____

   _____

4. Carlos _____

   _____

5. Jack and Jill_____

   _____

6. Lucy _____

   _____

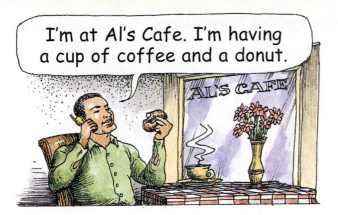

7. Grover _____

_____

8. Mr. and Mrs. Lee _____

_____

9. Maria _____

_____

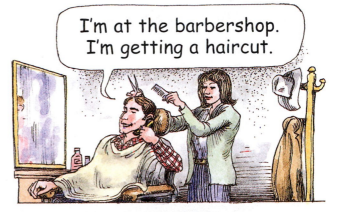

10. Dallas _____

_____

11. Ken and Suzi _____

_____

12. Mr. Gamble _____

_____

▶ **PRACTICE** • *Read out loud the sentences you wrote about the pictures.*

GRAMMAR REVIEW • Present Continuous

▶ **WHAT'S WRONG?** • *Correct the sentences about the pictures.*

1. A: Maynard is taking a bath.

   B: <u>He isn't taking a bath.</u>

   <u>He's taking a shower.</u>

2. A: The girls are playing basketball.

   B: <u>They aren't playing basketball.</u>

   <u>They're playing volleyball.</u>

3. A: Daisy is trying on a coat.

   B: _____

   _____

4. A: Lucy and Grover are buying a radio.

   B: _____

   _____

5. A: The men are having breakfast.

   B: _____

   _____

6. A: Dallas is talking with Maria.

   B: _____

   _____

7. A: Maria is reading a book.

   B: _____

   _____

8. A: Jack and Jill are going to the bank.

   B: _____

   _____

9. A: Mr. Denby is eating an orange.

   B: _____

   _____

10. A: Suzi is wearing a blue dress.

    B: _____

    _____

11. A: The boys are looking at a dog.

    B: _____

    _____

12. A: Carlos is repairing a car.

    B: _____

    _____

▶ **PAIR WORK** • *Practice the conversations.*

GRAMMAR REVIEW • Present Continuous

Who is she talking to?	A friend.
What is he looking at?	His dictionary.
Where are they studying?	At the library.

▶ 🎧 *Listen. Listen and repeat.*　　▶ **PAIR WORK** • *Practice the conversations.*

▶ **WRITING** • *Complete the questions using these verbs:* **dance (with), drink, eat, go, make, read, sleep, wait (for), write (to).**

Who <u>are they waiting for</u>?

Donna.

1.

Where _____?

On the sofa.

2.

What _____?

Lemonade.

3.

Where _____?

At Al's Cafe.

4.

Who _____?

Her boyfriend.

5.

What _____?

A sandwich.

6.

What _____?

The newspaper.

7.

Where _____?

To school.

8.

Who _____?

His family.

9.

GRAMMAR REVIEW • Adjectives

🎧 *Listen. Listen and repeat.*

▶ **PAIR WORK** • *Practice the conversations.*

1. A: Where's Alice?

   B: <u>She's in the kitchen.</u>

   A: Is she married or single?

   B: <u>She's married.</u>

   A: Is she busy?

   B: <u>Yes, she is.</u>

2. A: Where are the children?

   B: <u>They're at the park.</u>

   A: Are they quiet or noisy?

   B: <u>They're noisy.</u>

   A: Are they sad?

   B: <u>No, they aren't. They're happy.</u>

3. A: Where's Bruno?

   B: _____

   A: Is he handsome or ugly?

   B: _____

   A: Is he strong?

   B: _____

4. A: Where are the apples?

   B: _____

   A: Are they red or green?

   B: _____

   A: Are they small?

   B: _____

5. A: Where's Vanessa?

   B: _____

   A: Is she young or old?

   B: _____

   A: Is she a teacher?

   B: _____

6. A: Where's the library?

   B: _____

   A: Is it big or small?

   B: _____

   A: Is it old?

   B: _____

7. A: Where are the boys?

   B: _____

   A: Are they hot or cold?

   B: _____

   A: Are they thirsty?

   B: _____

8. A: Where's Mr. Grand?

   B: _____

   A: Is he rich or poor?

   B: _____

   A: Is he tall?

   B: _____

▶ **WRITING** • *Fill in the answers. Then read the conversations aloud.*

▶ 🎧 *Look and listen. Listen and repeat.*

▶ **PRACTICE** • *Give commands to other students in your class. Use the verbs*
(1) open, (2) close, (3) show, (4) give, (5) bring, (6) put *and the nouns in the box.*

Example: (1) open **Open the door.** OR **Open your dictionary.**

pen	ruler	book	magazine	table	door	watch
pencil	eraser	notebook	dictionary	bookcase	window	ring

Note: Use *please* to be more polite. ➞ Please open the door.

LIFE SKILL • Talking on the telephone

▶ 🎧 *Listen. Listen and practice.*

▶ **WRITING** • *Complete the sentences using the expressions in the box.*

cleaning the kitchen	listening to some CDs	playing with the dog
doing my homework	making dinner	relaxing in the backyard

▶ **PAIR WORK** • *Have conversations using the information in the pictures.*

A: **Hi, _____. Are you busy?**

B: **Yes, I'm _____. OR No, I'm just _____.**

READING

This is Richard Garcia. I'm reporting to you from the corner of Main Street and Third Avenue. I'm standing in front of the Majestic Apartments on a beautiful spring day. Right here I see some children washing their dog in a large bucket of water. The children are only about eight years old, but they're doing a good job of washing their dog. And they're having fun!

Down the street a young woman is talking to her boyfriend. They're standing next to a big motorcycle. Both of them are wearing leather jackets and blue jeans. They're holding hands, and they look happy.

Right behind me an elderly gentleman is walking up the steps. He's carrying a large bag of groceries. His wife is standing at the top of the steps. She's waiting for her husband, and she's smiling. He's probably bringing home some food for their dinner.

Well, this gives you an idea of what's happening today at the corner of Main Street and Third Avenue. I'm Richard Garcia reporting for KWIC News.

▶ STORY QUESTIONS

1. Where is Richard Garcia?
2. Is he reporting for a news station?
3. What are the children doing?
4. Are they having a good time?

PICTURE DICTATION

▶ **WRITING** • *Write 4 questions about the other people in the picture on page 74: The young woman and her boyfriend, the elderly gentleman and his wife.*

1. _____

2. _____

3. _____

4. _____

▶ **CLASS ACTIVITY** • *What's happening in the picture?*

▶ **WARM UP**

1. Where are the children?
2. What are they laughing at?
3. Where is the elderly woman?
4. What is she doing while she's waiting for the bus?
5. Do you think she looks elegant in her red dress?
6. Is the young man waving to his girlfriend?
7. What is he bringing her?

▶ 🎧 **DICTATION** • *Listen and write what you hear on a separate piece of paper.*

VOCABULARY

NOUNS

Places
barbershop
department store
flower shop
gas station
laundromat
market
theater
zoo

Other
aunt
bath
bills
bookcase
donut
feet
food
gentleman
girlfriend
groceries
hand
haircut
homework
idea
leather jacket
living room
motorcycle
notebook
pair
pen
ring
roses
ruler
sandwich
shower
volleyball
water

VERBS
clean
close
give
hold
make
move
pay
put
repair
show
try on
visit
wave

ADJECTIVES
busy
easy
elderly
elegant
funny

ADVERB
probably

DETERMINER
some

EXPRESSIONS

Asking for and giving location
Excuse me. I'm looking for…
    It's across the street.
      …down the street.
      …at the corner of…
      …right here.

Giving encouragement
I'm a little nervous.
    That's okay.
I'm not a very good dancer.
    Don't worry. You're doing fine.

Thanking someone
Thank you.
    You're welcome.

Complimenting
They're doing a good job.

Other
Welcome…
Are you ready?
Let's dance.

Come on.
Do your homework.
See how easy it is?
Uh, huh.

Like this?
That's better.
That's perfect.

PRONUNCIATION

▶ **A** 🎧 *Listen and repeat.*

/i/

1. this	4. give	7. sit
2. big	5. him	8. in
3. dish	6. dinner	9. kitchen

▶ **B** 🎧 *Listen and repeat.*

/iy/

1. see	4. sweet	7. weak
2. clean	5. peach	8. green
3. feet	6. tree	9. tea

▶ **C** 🎧 *Listen to each pair of words. Listen and repeat.*

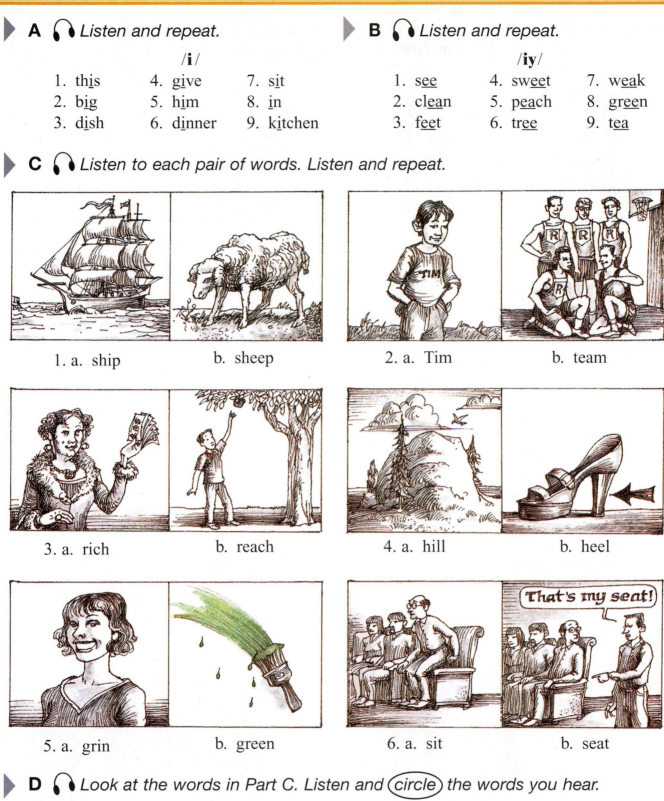

1. a. ship b. sheep

2. a. Tim b. team

3. a. rich b. reach

4. a. hill b. heel

5. a. grin b. green

6. a. sit b. seat

That's my seat!

▶ **D** 🎧 *Look at the words in Part C. Listen and* (circle) *the words you hear.*

▶ **E** 🎧 *Listen and practice.*

1. Jim is eating a big peach.
2. Please clean this window.
3. See how easy it is?
4. Nick is reading his magazine.
5. We live on Hill Street.
6. Please visit me this week.

TEST

1. a. Hello there.
   b. How are you?
   c. What's your name?
   d. What are you doing?

2. a. That's good.
   b. Thank you.
   c. You're welcome.
   d. Nice to meet you.

3. "Where is Mr. Denby?"
   "_____ in the classroom."

   a. He's   c. You're
   b. She's   d. It's

4. "Where are the pencils?"
   "_____ in the desk."

   a. It's   c. They're
   b. They   d. Those

5. "_____ is that man?"
   "His name is Mike Kelly."

   a. What   c. Who
   b. Where   d. How

6. "_____ is Ms. Adams?"
   "She's at the office."

   a. What   c. Who
   b. Where   d. How

7. "How much is that dress?"
   "It's _____."

   a. small   c. beautiful
   b. for sale   d. fifty dollars

8. "What time is it?"
   "It's ten _____."

   a. o'clock   c. hours
   b. minutes   d. years old

9. a. this   c. these
   b. that   d. those

10. a. This   c. These
    b. That   d. Those

11. Nick is standing _____ his car.

   a. on   c. behind

   b. next to   d. in front of

12. The bank is _____ the hotel.

   a. on   c. behind

   b. next to   d. in front of

13. The radio is _____ the living room.

   a. in   c. at

   b. on   d. of

14. What's the color _____ your kitchen?

   a. at   c. of

   b. on   d. to

15. "_____"

"It's sunny and warm."

   a. Are you comfortable?

   b. How's the weather?

   c. What's your favorite season?

   d. When is summer?

16. "_____ Where's the library?"

"It's on Central Avenue."

   a. Ask me.

   b. Listen to me.

   c. Talk to me.

   d. Excuse me.

17. My _____ is 673 Maple Street.

   a. address   c. house

   b. business   d. phone number

18. Lucy is making spaghetti for _____ _____.

   a. food   c. dinner

   b. eat   d. hungry

19. "Are Jack and Jill at the park?"

"_____"

   a. Yes, they are.   c. Yes, he is.

   b. No, they aren't.   d. No, she isn't.

20. "Is Maynard sleeping?"

"_____"

   a. Yes, he is.   c. Yes, I am.

   b. No, he isn't.   d. No, they aren't.

_____ the window!

Don't _____ on the grass.

21. a. Open   c. Don't open
    b. Close   d. Don't close

22. a. sit   c. walk
    b. stand   d. run

23. That computer isn't old.
It's _____.
    a. new   c. cheap
    b. young   d. good

24. Is Mr. Grand rich or _____?
    a. short   c. good
    b. happy   d. poor

25. My friends _____ the beach.
    a. is going   c. are going to
    b. are going   d. are going for

26. Grover _____ lunch.
    a. is taking   c. is drinking
    b. is eating   d. are having

27. Maria and I are busy.
Don't talk to _____ now.
    a. us   c. her
    b. them   d. me

28. The man is hungry.
Give _____ some food.
    a. he   c. his
    b. her   d. him

Are you enjoying _____ dinner?

29. a. my   c. his
    b. your   d. her

_____ name is John.

30. a. My   c. Her
    b. Your   d. His

 TOPICS

People

Cars

Family relationships

GRAMMAR

have

Possessive adjectives

Possessive nouns

FUNCTIONS

Talking about family members

Describing people's appearance and personality

Making phone calls

PRONUNCIATION

/æ/ vs. /e/

Chapter

CARTOON STORY

GRAMMAR • To Have

Yes/No Question	Short Answers	
Do you have a big family?	Yes, I do.	No, I don't.

▶ **PAIR WORK** • *Ask and answer questions.*

1. a big family
A: **Do you have a big family?**
B: **Yes, I do.** OR **No, I don't.**

1. a big family

2. a garden

3. a garage

4. a fireplace

5. a lamp

6. a bookcase

7. a computer

8. a wallet

9. a driver's license

GRAMMAR • To Have

Affirmative		
He She	has	a computer.

Word Bank			
bicycle	clothes dryer	violin	wallet
motorcycle	washing machine	guitar	handbag

▶ 🎧 *Look and listen.*   ▶ **WRITING** • *Write a sentence for each picture.*

1. <u>She has a washing machine.</u>   2. <u>He has a clothes dryer.</u>

3. _____   4. _____   5. _____

6. _____   7. _____   8. _____

▶ **PRACTICE** • *Read the sentences out loud.*

GRAMMAR • To Have

Negative		
He She	doesn't (does not)	have a job.

Word Bank			
car	watch	umbrella	bookcase
lamp	coat	girlfriend	driver's license

▶ 🎧 *Look and listen.* ▶ **WRITING** • *Write a negative sentence for each picture.*

1. <u>She doesn't have a driver's license.</u>   2. <u>He doesn't have a girlfriend.</u>

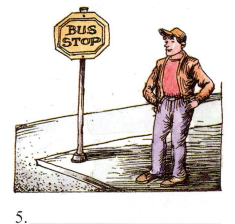

3. _____   4. _____   5. _____

6. _____   7. _____   8. _____

_____   _____   _____

▶ **PRACTICE** • *Read the sentences out loud.*

GRAMMAR • To Have

Yes/No Question			
Does	he she	have	a dictionary?

Short Answers					
Yes,	he she	does.	No,	he she	doesn't.

▶ **PAIR WORK** • *Ask and answer questions.*

1. A: **Does Dallas have a wallet?**
   B: **Yes, he does.**

2. A: **Does Daisy have a wallet?**
   B: **No, she doesn't. She has a handbag.**

3. Does Ken have a computer?

4. Does Jill have an orange?

5. Does Maria have a violin?

6. Does Carlos have a violin?

7. Does Becky have a dog?

8. Does Grover have a motorcycle?

9. Does Lucy have a motorcycle?

GRAMMAR • To Have

Affirmative	Negative
They have a radio.	They don't have a television.

▶ 🎧 *Listen to Mr. and Mrs. Kilbride.*

We don't have a television.

So we sit on the porch and listen to the radio.

▶ **WRITING** • *Write affirmative and negative sentences about Mr. and Mrs. Kilbride. After you finish, read the sentences out loud.*

1. (radio) __They have a radio.__

2. (television) __They don't have a television.__

3. (car) _____

4. (motorcycle) _____

5. (garage) _____

6. (apple tree) _____

7. (garden) _____

8. (porch) _____

9. (dog) _____

10. (cat) _____

11. (clothes dryer) _____

12. (fireplace) _____

GRAMMAR • To Have

Yes/No Question	Short Answers	
Do they have a computer?	Yes, they do.	No, they don't.

▶ **PAIR WORK** • *Ask and answer questions.*

1. a washing machine
A: **Do they have a washing machine?**
B: **Yes, they do.**

2. a clothes dryer
A: **Do they have a clothes dryer?**
B: **No, they don't.**

3. a television

4. a bookcase

5. a radio

6. money

7. jobs

8. a garden

9. a car

CAR TALK

▶ 🎧 *Listen. Listen and practice.*

POSSESSIVE ADJECTIVES

I like **my** car.	He likes **his** car.	We like **our** car.
You like **your** car.	She likes **her** car.	They like **their** car.

GRAMMAR • Possessive Adjectives

🎧 *Listen. Listen and repeat.*   ▶ **PAIR WORK** • *Practice the conversations.*

▶ **WRITING** • *Complete the conversations using these words:*

this that these those	my your his her our their

1. Whose sandwich is this?
It's your sandwich.

2. Whose chickens are those?
They're our chickens.

3. _____ sunglasses _____?
They're _____.

4. _____ bicycle _____?
It's _____.

5. _____ ball _____?
It's _____.

6. _____ pictures _____?
They're _____.

_____ flowers _____?

They're _____.

⑦

_____ cat _____?

It's _____.

⑧

_____ envelopes _____?

They're _____.

⑨

_____ cell phone _____?

It's _____.

⑩

_____ dog _____?

It's _____.

⑪

_____ books _____?

They're _____.

⑫

▶ **PAIR WORK** • *Read the conversations aloud.*

GRAMMAR • Possessive Nouns

▶ 🎧 *Listen. Listen and practice.*

Do you like Milton's green tie?

No, I don't like green very much.

Do you like the girls' blue uniforms?

Yes, I think blue is a beautiful color.

▶ **PAIR WORK** • *Look at the pictures and talk about the people's clothing.*

1. Ken's brown jacket
A: **Do you like Ken's brown jacket?**
B: **Yes, I think brown is a great color. OR No, I don't like brown very much.**

1. Ken's brown jacket

2. Maria's green dress

3. the boys' orange T-shirts

4. Susan's blue pants

5. Joe's purple shirt

6. the ladies' pink gloves

7. the men's black hats

8. Lucy's yellow blouse

9. Mr. Denby's gray sweater

FAMILY RELATIONSHIPS

▶ 🎧 *Listen and repeat.*

THE ADAMS FAMILY

① father
② mother
③ son
④ daughter
⑤ husband
⑥ wife
⑦ brother
⑧ sister

▶ **WRITING** • *Complete the sentences. Then read the sentences out loud.*

1. Ryan is Tom's ___son___ .
2. Tom is Ryan's _____ .
3. Becky is Linda's _____ .
4. Linda is Becky's _____ .
5. Tom is Linda's _____ .
6. Linda is Tom's _____ .
7. Ryan is Becky's _____ .
8. Becky is Ryan's _____ .

▶ 🎧 *Listen. Listen and practice.*

MARIA: Tell me about your family, Carlos.
          Do you have any brothers or sisters?

CARLOS: I have a brother and a sister.

MARIA: Oh, really? What are their names?

CARLOS: My brother's name is Luis, and my
          sister's name is Ana.

MARIA: So you have five people in
          your family.

CARLOS: That's right. How many people do
          you have in your family?

MARIA: Eight. I have two brothers and
          three sisters.

CARLOS: Wow! You have a big family.

▶ **PAIR WORK** • *Have similar conversations about your families. How many brothers and sisters do you have? What are their names?*

DESCRIBING PEOPLE • Appearance

▶ 🎧 *Listen. Listen and repeat.*

Stanley is tall. ⑥

Bill is average height. ⑤

Richard is short. ④

Jan has blond hair. ①

Sue has brown hair. ②

Rita has black hair. ③

Mrs. Lee is in her thirties. ⑧

Mr. Lee is in his forties. ⑨

Emma Lee is thirteen. ⑦

▶ **WRITING** • *Describe the people at the picnic.*

1. He's tall, he has blond hair, and he's about thirty-five.

2. _____

3. _____

4. _____

5. _____

6. _____

7. _____

▶ **PRACTICE** • *Describe someone in your family.*

▶ 🎧 *Look and listen. Listen and repeat.*

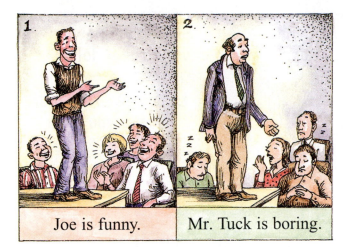

Joe is funny.	Mr. Tuck is boring.

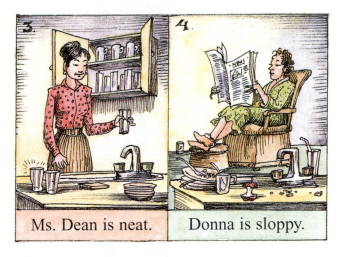

Ms. Dean is neat.	Donna is sloppy.

Lucy is talkative.	Annabelle is shy.

Al is hardworking.	Fred is lazy.

▶ **WRITING** • *Describe five people who are important to you. Use the best adjective to describe each person.*

Example: <u>My brother is sloppy.</u>

1. _____

2. _____

3. _____

4. _____

5. _____

IMPORTANT PEOPLE			
mother	sister	girlfriend	aunt
father	brother	boyfriend	uncle

ADJECTIVES			
funny	boring	talkative	shy
neat	sloppy	hardworking	lazy

▶ **PAIR WORK** • *Use two or three adjectives to describe your best friend.*

A: **What's your best friend like?**
B: **She's talkative, very funny and a little lazy.**

a little

very

CARTOON STORY

🎧 *Jason is looking for a pay phone. Listen. Listen and practice.*

▶ **STORY QUESTIONS** • *Look at the pictures for the answers.*

1. Where is Jason? What's he looking for?
2. What is Jason's problem?
3. Does the old man have change for a dollar?
4. Why is Jason calling the operator?
5. What is Pat's phone number?
6. Look at the lady with the red hair. Why is she angry with Jason?
7. What does Jason say to the lady?

CARTOON STORY

► **STORY QUESTIONS (continued)** • *Look at the pictures for the answers.*

8. What does the girl in the green sweater ask Jason?
9. What is Jason doing while she's talking on the phone?
10. What does the girl say after using the phone?
11. Is Pat home the first time Jason calls? Where is she?
12. Is Jason looking at his watch? What's he doing?
13. Is Pat home now?
14. What is Pat wearing?
15. What is Pat doing while she's talking with Jason?
16. How does Jason feel? Is he sad or angry?

VOCABULARY

NOUNS

Family Members

mother
father
wife
husband
brother
sister
son
daughter

Other

chicken
clothes dryer
driver's license
envelope
fireplace
garage
guitar
hair

handbag
lamp
oil
violin
wallet
washing machine

VERB

sell

ADJECTIVES

boring
cute
funny
hardworking
lazy
lucky
neat
sloppy
talkative
top

POSSESSIVE ADJECTIVES

our
their

DETERMINER

any

CONJUNCTION

so

EXPRESSIONS

Describing people

He's tall.
  …short.
  …average-height.
She has blond hair.
She's in her thirties.
She's about thirty-five.

Talking about cars

How do you like our new car?
  I like it very much.
She takes good care of her car.
  That's for sure.
Your car is in bad shape.
  What's wrong with it?

Asking for a phone number

What city?
  Maywood. I'd like the number of Pat Lacy.
How do you spell the last name?
  L-A-C-Y.
The number is 473-2906.
  Thank you.

Getting the wrong number

Hello. Is Pat there?
  No, you have the wrong number.
Is this 473-2906?
  No, it isn't.
I'm sorry.

Asking to speak with someone

Hello. Can I speak to Pat, please?
  Pat isn't here right now. She's at work.
Hello. Is Pat there now?
  Yes, she is. Just a minute, please.

Talking on the phone

Hi, Pat. This is Jason Brown.
  Oh, hi, Jason.
What are you doing?
  I'm watching my favorite TV show.
  Can you call me later?

Other

May I use the phone?
Oh, no…I don't have any change.
This isn't my day.

I'm finished.
Oh, really?
That's right.

It's over there.
Wow!
What a nice house!

Let's see…
Here you are.
Thanks.

PRONUNCIATION

A 🎧 *Listen and repeat.*

/æ/

1. fat	4. that	7. sad
2. black	5. bad	8. happy
3. cat	6. apple	9. pants

B 🎧 *Listen and repeat.*

/e/

1. ten	4. sell	7. heavy
2. yes	5. red	8. yellow
3. men	6. dress	9. sweater

C 🎧 *Listen to each pair of words. Listen again and repeat.*

1. a. pan   b. pen   2. a. man   b. men

3. a. Jan   b. Jen   4. a. tan   b. ten

5. a. gas   b. guess   6. a. bad   b. bed

D 🎧 *Look at the words in Part C. Listen and* (circle) *the words you hear.*

E 🎧 *Listen and practice.*

1. Jen has a red hat.
2. The happy chef is at his desk.
3. My best friend is an acrobat.
4. The men are standing next to the bank.
5. Texas is having bad weather.
6. Is Dan ready for the next dance?

GRAMMAR SUMMARY

TO HAVE Affirmative

He She	has	
I You We They	have	a car.

Negative

He She	doesn't (does not)	
I You We They	don't (do not)	have a car.

Interrogative

Does	he she	
Do	I you we they	have a car?

Short Answers

Yes,	he she	does.	No,	he she	doesn't.
	I you we they	do.		I you we they	don't.

POSSESSIVE ADJECTIVES

It's	my your his her our their	house.

Questions with WHOSE

Whose	radio is that? books are those?

POSSESSIVE NOUNS

It's John's radio.

They're the girls' books.

CONTENTS

▶ **TOPICS**

Apartments

Furniture and rooms

Food

Eating habits

▶ **GRAMMAR**

There is / there are

Some / any

Countables / uncountables

like, want, need

▶ **FUNCTIONS**

Asking about and describing apartments

Buying furniture

Expressing preferences in food

Ordering fast food

Shopping for food

Asking a favor

▶ **PRONUNCIATION**

/ɑ/ vs. /ʌ/

Chapter

6

CARTOON STORY

▶ 🎧 *Listen. Listen and practice.*

▶ **STORY QUESTIONS**

1. Does Carlos live on the top floor of his apartment building?
2. Is there an elevator in the building? Is it working?
3. How is Mrs. Jones today? What does she need?
4. How is the view from Carlos' apartment?
5. Is Maria hungry? What's in the refrigerator?
6. Is there some coffee on the stove? Where are the coffee cups?
7. What does Maria see in the window? What's it doing?

▶ 🎧 *Listen and repeat.*

There's a bird in the window.   There's a lamp on the table.
_____ computer on the desk.   _____ newspaper on the bed.
_____ mirror on the wall.   _____ dog under the bed.

Yes/No Question	Short Answers	
Is there a telephone in the bedroom?	Yes, there is.	No, there isn't.

▶ **PRACTICE** • *Answer the teacher; then ask each other these questions.*

A: **Is there a mirror on the wall?**   A: **Is there a picture on the wall?**
B: **Yes, there is.**   B: **No, there isn't.**

1. Is there a lamp on the table?   5. Is there a dog under the bed?
2. Is there a clock on the table?   6. Is there a telephone on the desk?
3. Is there a magazine on the bed?   7. Is there a computer on the desk?
4. Is there a newspaper on the bed?   8. Is there a dictionary on the desk?

▶ **PAIR WORK** • *Ask if these items are in your partner's bedroom.*

Example: clock
Student A: **Is there a clock in your bedroom?**
Student B: **Yes, there is. OR No, there isn't.**

1. clock   4. piano   7. lamp
2. radio   5. television   8. desk
3. telephone   6. computer   9. mirror

▶ 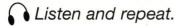 *Listen and repeat.*

There are some apples in the bowl.   There are some bottles on the table.

_____ dishes in the sink.   _____ cups on the shelf.

_____ spoons on the counter.   _____ pots on the wall.

knives

forks

spoons

Yes/No Question	Short Answers	
Are there any chairs in the kitchen?	Yes, there are.	No, there aren't.

▶ **PRACTICE** • *Answer the teacher; then ask each other these questions.*

A: **Are there any dishes in the sink?**   A: **Are there any pots in the sink?**
B: **Yes, there are.**   B: **No, there aren't.**

1. Are there any pots on the wall?   5. Are there any glasses on the shelf?
2. Are there any oranges in the bowl?   6. Are there any spoons on the counter?
3. Are there any apples in the bowl?   7. Are there any knives on the counter?
4. Are there any cups on the shelf?   8. Are there any dishes on the table?

▶ **PAIR WORK** • *Ask if these items are in your partner's kitchen.*

Example: pots
Student A: **Are there any pots in your kitchen?**
Student B: **Yes, there are.** OR **No, there aren't.**

1. flowers   4. books   7. cups
2. apples   5. chairs   8. bottles
3. oranges   6. pots   9. magazines

LIFE SKILL • Buying Furniture

🎧 *Listen. Listen and practice.*

PAIR WORK • *Have similar conversations.*

1. lamp / $75

2. table / $330

3. chair / $139

4. desk / $265

A: May I help you?

B: Yes. I need a _____.

A: The _____ are over there. Do you see one you like?

B: Yes. I like this one. How much is it?

A: _____.

B: Good. I'll take it.
   OR   Oh, that's too expensive.

5. armchair / $550

6. sofa / $898

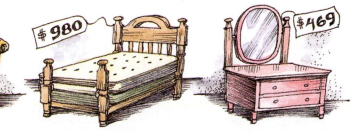

7. bed / $980

8. dresser / $469

▶ **WRITING** • *Give the location of these objects.*

1. (pictures) <u>There are some pictures in the living room.</u>
2. (dresser) <u>There's a dresser in the bedroom.</u>
3. (stove)_____
4. (books) _____
5. (mirror)_____
6. (pots) _____
7. (flowers)_____
8. (piano) _____

▶ **PAIR WORK** • *Ask and answer questions.*

      chairs / kitchen   piano / bedroom
A: **Are there any chairs in the kitchen?**   A: **Is there a piano in the bedroom?**
B: **Yes, there are.**   B: **No, there isn't.**

1. piano / living room   4. mirror / bathroom   7. window / bathroom
2. flowers / living room   5. mirror / bedroom   8. pictures / living room
3. flowers / bedroom   6. pots / kitchen   9. pictures / bedroom

GRAMMAR • Countables and Uncountables

▶ 🎧 **BASIC FOOD GROUPS** • *Look and listen. Listen and repeat.*

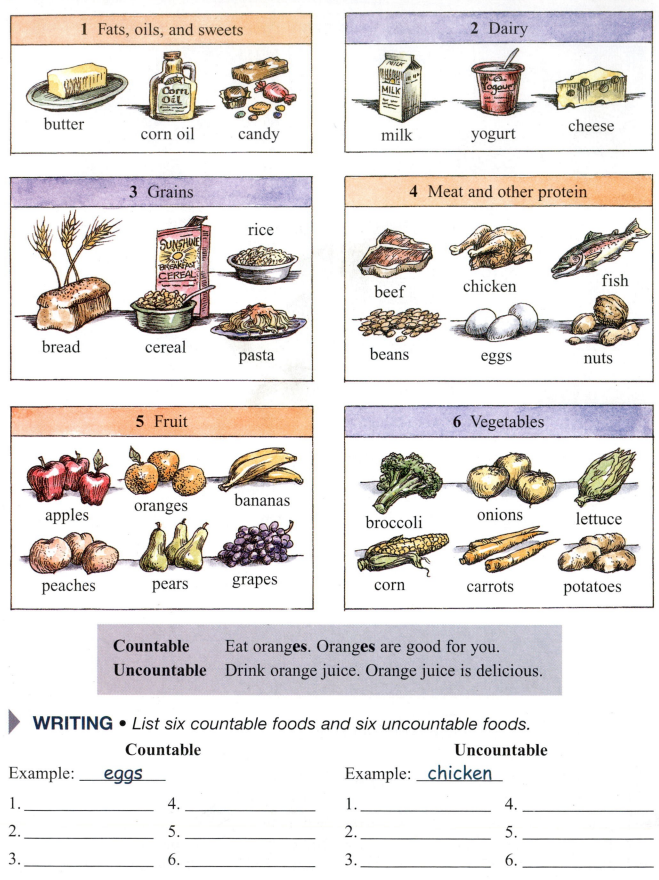

1 Fats, oils, and sweets

butter   corn oil   candy

2 Dairy

milk   yogurt   cheese

3 Grains

rice

bread   cereal   pasta

4 Meat and other protein

beef   chicken   fish

beans   eggs   nuts

5 Fruit

apples   oranges   bananas

peaches   pears   grapes

6 Vegetables

broccoli   onions   lettuce

corn   carrots   potatoes

Countable	Eat orang**es**. Orang**es** are good for you.
Uncountable	Drink orange juice. Orange juice is delicious.

▶ **WRITING** • *List six countable foods and six uncountable foods.*

Countable	Uncountable
Example: ___eggs___	Example: ___chicken___

1._____	4._____	1._____	4._____
2._____	5._____	2._____	5._____
3._____	6._____	3._____	6._____

GRAMMAR • Partitives

▶ 🎧 *Listen and repeat.*

| can | jar | bottle | bag | box |

▶ **WRITING** • *Fill in the blanks with **bottle, jar, can, bag, box,** or **bunch**.*

1. a __bottle__ of water

2. a __bunch__ of grapes

3. a _____ of soup

4. a _____ of cereal

5. a _____ of olives

6. a _____ of cookies

7. a _____ of ketchup

8. a _____ of chocolates

9. a _____ of bananas

10. a _____ of mustard

11. a _____ of beans

12. a _____ of potatoes

There's a	bowl of soup on the table.
There are some	sandwiches on the table.
There's some	mustard next to the sandwiches.

▶ **NOTE** • We say **there's some mustard**, not ~~there are some mustard~~. Mustard is uncountable.

▶ **WRITING** • *Complete the sentences using* **There's a**, **There are some**, *or* **There's some**.

1. <u>There's a</u> plate of spaghetti on the table.
2. <u>There's some</u> tomato sauce on the spaghetti.
3. _____ glasses on the table.
4. _____ bottle of water next to the glasses.
5. _____ fruit on the table.
6. _____ dishes on the table.
7. _____ cookbook on the counter.
8. _____ lettuce on the counter.
9. _____ tomatoes next to the lettuce.
10. _____ coffee on the stove.

▶ **PRACTICE** • *Read the sentences out loud.*

GRAMMAR • Countables/Uncountables: Negative

There isn't any	soup left.

There aren't any	more sandwiches.

▶ **WRITING** • *Complete with* **There isn't any** *or* **There aren't any.**

I'm sorry. <u>There aren't any</u> bananas left.

1. Susan and the grocer

Sorry, Jinx. <u>There isn't any</u> more milk.

2. Max and Jinx

_____ gas stations around here.

3. The mailman and Daisy

I'm sorry. _____ roses left.

4. Miss Brady and Dallas

_____ water left.

5. Jane and Milton

_____ more cookies.

6. Jimmy and his mom

ACE Employment Agency

I'm sorry. _____ jobs for clowns.

7. Bobo and Ms. Grimes

Ben's Ice Cream Parlor

I'm sorry. _____ more chocolate.

8. Lucy and Ben

Singles' Party

_____ good men left.

9. Candy and Rosie

▶ 🎧 *Listen to the conversations.*

CARTOON STORY

Becky and her mother are shopping at the neighborhood market. Listen. Listen and practice.

▶ **STORY QUESTIONS**

1. Where are Becky and her mother?
2. What does Becky want for dinner?
3. What do they need to make spaghetti?
4. Where is the tomato sauce?
5. Do they need any onions?
6. What about garlic?

▶ **DISCUSSION QUESTIONS**

1. Where do you shop for food?
2. What foods do you buy there?
3. Do they have everything you need?
4. What fruits are in season now?
5. What's your favorite fruit?
6. How much is a bunch of bananas?

▶ 🎧 *Listen. Listen and practice.*

Do you like grapes?

How's the coffee?

Do you like chocolate cake?

Do you like strawberries?

They're okay.

It's delicious.

Yes, of course. Everyone likes chocolate cake.

Yes, very much.

Do you like cheese?

No, not very much.

▶ **PAIR WORK** • *Talk about these foods.*

No, not at all.

1. chicken

A: **Do you like chicken?**
B: **Yes, of course.**
   OR **It's okay.**
   OR **No, not very much.**

2. French fries

A: **Do you like French fries?**
B: **Yes, very much.**
   OR **They're okay.**
   OR **No, not at all.**

1. chicken

2. French fries

3. pizza

4. mushrooms

5. coffee

6. peanuts

7. cheese

8. hot dogs

LIFE SKILL • Reading Advertisements

Save $$ this week! JUNIOR'S MARKET $$ sale! $$

1. T-Bone STEAK $5.⁹⁰ lb.
2. AVOCADOS 99¢ each
3. Florida ORANGE JUICE 32 ounce carton $1.⁶⁹
4. Sponge MOPS $6.²⁵ each
5. TOMATOES 88¢ lb.
6. Sparkle Detergent $7.⁸⁵
7. Bandera BANANAS 39¢ lb.
8. Scrubb Toothbrushes • selected types • $1.⁷⁹ each
9. In our bakery BREAD $2.⁹⁹

▶ **WRITING** • *Answer the questions about the items on sale this week at Junior's Market.*

1. How much is the T-bone steak? <u>It's five dollars and ninety cents a pound.</u>
2. How much are the avocados? <u>They're ninety-nine cents each.</u>
3. How much is the orange juice? <u>It's a dollar sixty-nine.</u>
4. How much are the sponge mops? _____
5. How much are the tomatoes? _____
6. How much is the detergent? _____
7. How much are the bananas? _____
8. How much are the toothbrushes? _____
9. How much is the bread? _____

▶ **PAIR WORK** • *Ask and answer questions about the items that are on sale this week.*

LIFE SKILL • Shopping for Food

▶ 🎧 *Listen. Listen and practice.*

LUCY: Can you do me a favor?

GROVER: Sure.

LUCY: I need some things at the store.

GROVER: What do you need?

LUCY: Some apples, chicken soup and a quart of milk.

GROVER: Let's see…apples, chicken soup and a quart of milk.

LUCY: That's right.

GROVER: Anything else?

LUCY: Yes! Some laundry detergent. Get Sparkle. It's on sale.

GROVER: Okay.

LUCY: Thanks, Grover.

GROVER: No problem.

▶ **WRITING** • *Make a list of five things you need at the store. After you finish, pair up and have a conversation like the one above.*

LIFE SKILL • Ordering Fast Food

▶ 🎧 *Listen and repeat.*

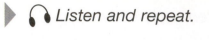

MENU

1. hamburger	2. chicken sandwich	3. salad	4. French fries

DRINKS

5. soda	6. orange juice	7. coffee	8. milk

DESSERTS

9. ice cream	10. apple pie	11. chocolate cake	12. cookies

▶ 🎧 *Listen. Listen and practice.*

A: Can I help you?

B: Yes. I'd like a hamburger.

A: Do you want everything on it? Lettuce, onions and tomato?

B: Yes. I'd also like a coffee and some apple pie.

A: Okay. Anything else?

B: No, that's all.

▶ **PAIR WORK** • *Have similar conversations. Order anything from the menu above.*

TOPIC • Eating Habits

▶ 🎧 *Listen and read.*

Every day Jimmy eats lunch at the school cafeteria. Today he's having a cheeseburger with French fries, an apple, a cherry soda, and a piece of chocolate cake. Jimmy has a big appetite.

No, thank you.

Mrs. Wellington likes to eat in fancy restaurants. Today she's having grilled salmon, string beans, and a baked potato for lunch. She doesn't want anything for dessert because she doesn't like sweets.

Dallas is having a barbecue in his backyard. He's cooking chicken and steaks on the grill. Dallas loves spicy food, so he puts hot sauce on everything.

Jane is a vegetarian, so she doesn't eat any meat. She thinks the most nutritious foods are fruits and vegetables. Right now, Jane is making a salad for lunch.

▶ ## QUESTIONS

1. In your opinion, who's having the best lunch today?
2. Is it more fun to eat at home, in a restaurant, or outdoors?
3. What kind of foods do you like?
4. Do you like spicy foods?
5. What foods are best for your health?
6. What foods are not good for you?
7. Do you like desserts? Do you have a "sweet tooth"?
8. What's your favorite dessert?

VOCABULARY

NOUNS

Fruit
grape(s)
strawberries

Vegetables
broccoli
corn
green bean(s)
lettuce
potato(es)
tomato(es)

Dairy foods
butter
cheese
milk
yogurt

Grains
bread
cereal
pasta
rice

Meat/Protein
beef
eggs
fish
nuts

Fast foods
French fries
hamburger
pizza

Beverages
milk
orange juice
soda

Desserts
apple pie
chocolate cake
cookies
ice cream

Other food items
baked potato
garlic
mushrooms
salad
salmon
steak
tomato sauce

Rooms
bathroom
bedroom
kitchen

Furniture
armchair
bed
dresser

Other
aisle
appetite
bag
barbecue
bottle
box
building
can
counter

detergent
elevator
every day
floor
fork
grill
jar
knife
mirror
pot

refrigerator
shelf
sink
sponge mop
spoon
stove
toothbrush
vacation
vegetarian

PRONOUNS
everyone
everything

VERBS
cook
get
hope
know
live
need
want

ADJECTIVES
delicious
fancy
nutritious
spicy

ADVERBS
also
then

EXPRESSIONS

Shopping

May I help you?
   Yes. How much is…?
Twenty-five dollars.
   I'll take it.

Ordering fast food

May I help you?
   Yes, I'd like…
Anything else?
   No, that's all.

Talking about likes and dislikes

Do you like…?
   Yes, of course.
   Yes, very much.
   No, not very much.
   No, not at all.

Asking for a favor

Can you do me a favor?
   Sure.

Asking for and giving an opinion

How do you like the view?
   It's fantastic!

Talking about quantity

There isn't any milk left.
There aren't any more cookies.

Do you want sugar in your coffee?
   Yes, a little.

Describing a condition

The elevator isn't working.

Other

I hope…
I'm glad…

What about…?
Absolutely.

Very good.
No problem.

PRONUNCIATION

▶ **A** 🎧 *Listen and repeat.*

/ɑ/

1. top
2. box
3. shop
4. sloppy
5. hot
6. pot
7. want
8. father
9. doctor

▶ **B** 🎧 *Listen and repeat.*

/ʌ/

1. under
2. lunch
3. truck
4. some
5. funny
6. money
7. lucky
8. young
9. mother

▶ **C** 🎧 *Listen to each pair of words. Listen again and repeat.*

1. a. cop   b. cup

2. a. hot   b. hut

3. a. cot   b. cut

4. a. lock   b. luck

5. a. dock   b. duck

6. a. hog   b. hug

▶ **D** 🎧 *Look at the words in Part C. Listen and ⊙circle the words you hear.*

▶ **E** 🎧 *Listen and practice.*

1. The young cop is at the bus stop.
2. Your ugly socks are under the box.
3. Does Bob want a cup of coffee?
4. My brother loves hot popcorn.
5. Mother and father are watching us.
6. A long hot summer is not funny.

GRAMMAR SUMMARY

THERE IS / THERE ARE Affirmative		
There's (There is)	a dish	
There are	some cups	on the table.
There's (There is)	some cake	

Negative		
There isn't (There is not)	a dish	
There aren't (There are not)	any cups	on the table.
There isn't (There is not)	any cake	

Interrogative		
Is there	a dish	
Are there	any cups	on the table?
Is there	any cake	

Short Answers					
Yes,	there is.		No,	there isn't.	
	there are.			there aren't.	
	there is.			there isn't.	

TO LIKE Affirmative		
He She	likes	
I You We They	like	chocolate.

Negative		
He She	doesn't (does not)	
I You We They	don't (do not)	like chocolate.

Interrogative		
Does	he she	
Do	I you we they	like chocolate?

Short Answers					
Yes,	he she	does.	No,	he she	doesn't.
	I you we they	do.		I you we they	don't.

CONTENTS

 TOPICS

Daily routines

Music

Movies and television

 GRAMMAR

Simple present tense

 FUNCTIONS

Describing daily habits and routines

Talking about popular entertainment

 PRONUNCIATION

Verbs: different sounds for the *–s* ending

Chapter 7

CARTOON STORY

Jason is going to a dating service called Grand Expectations. He has an appointment with the president, Lotta Bagonia. Listen. Listen and practice.

QUESTIONS

1. Why is Jason going to a dating service?
2. Who is Lotta Bagonia?
3. Does Jason like the pictures of the new members? What does he say?
4. What does Jason do for a living?
5. What does he do in his free time?
6. What kind of music does Jason like?
7. Where does Jason take dancing lessons?
8. What kind of women does Jason like?
9. Does Jason become a member of Grand Expectations? Why or why not?

GRAMMAR • Simple Present Tense

▶ 🎧 *Listen as Luis talks about his daily routine. Listen and repeat.*

1. I get up at 6 o'clock.
2. I take a shower.
3. I get dressed.
4. I eat a big breakfast.
5. I brush my teeth.
6. I leave the house at 7:30.
7. I take the bus to school.
8. I have lunch in the cafeteria.
9. I come home at 4 o'clock.
10. I do my homework.
11. I have dinner with my family.
12. I go to bed at 10.

▶ 🎧 *Listen. Listen and practice.*

▶ **WRITING** • *Answer the following questions about your daily routine.*

1. When do you get up in the morning? <u>I get up at...</u>
2. What do you have for breakfast? _____
3. When do you leave the house? _____
4. How do you get to school/work? _____
5. Where do you have lunch? _____
6. When do you come home? _____
7. What do you do in the evening? _____
8. When do you go to bed? _____

▶ **PAIR WORK** • *Ask your partner five questions about his or her daily routine.*

GRAMMAR • Simple Present Tense

▶ 🎧 *Look and listen. Listen again and repeat.*

I get up early in the morning. I don't sleep late.

(1)

I drive to work. I don't take the bus.

(2)

I walk to work. I don't have a car.

(3)

I work fast. I don't waste time.

(4)

I exercise every day. I don't sit in front of a TV.

(5)

I only eat foods that are good for me. I don't like junk food.

(6)

▶ **PRACTICE** • *Read out loud the statements of each character on pages 126-127.*

Yes/No Question	Short Answers	
Do you get up early?	Yes, I do.	No, I don't.

▶ **PAIR WORK** • *Ask and answer questions.*

play the piano
A: **Do you play the piano?**
B: **Yes, I do.** OR **No, I don't.**

1. get up early
2. walk to school/work
3. sleep late on Saturday
4. exercise every day
5. eat junk food
6. like French fries
7. study a lot
8. relax on the weekend
9. watch a lot of TV

GRAMMAR • Simple Present Tense

Where	does	he she	live? work?	He She	lives works	in Hollywood.	Irregular: go - goes

▶ 🎧 *Listen. Listen and repeat.*

▶ **PAIR WORK** • *Practice the conversations.*

▶ **WRITING** • *Fill in the answers. Then read the conversations aloud.*

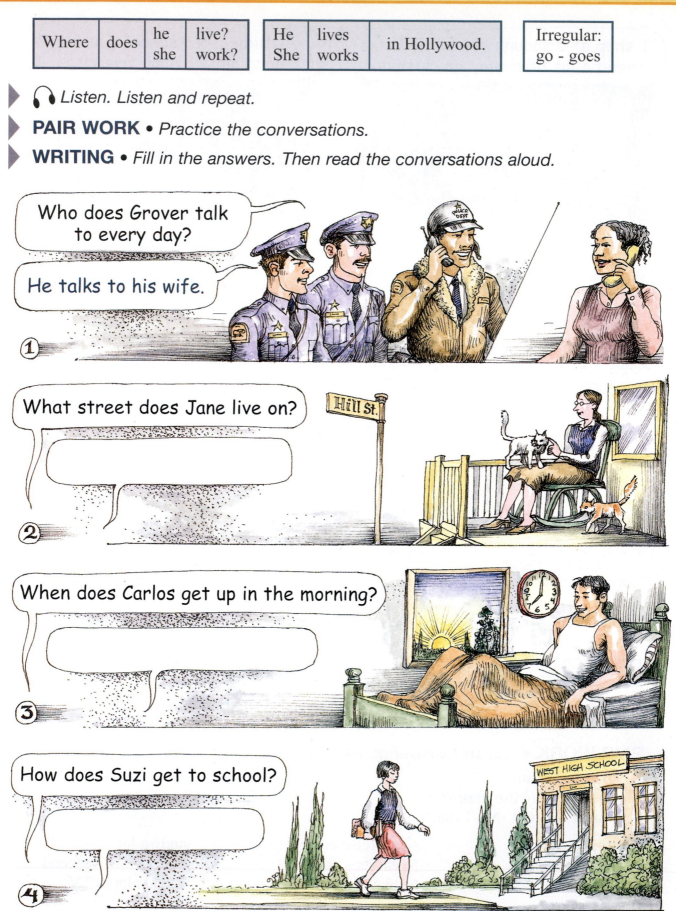

1. Who does Grover talk to every day?

   He talks to his wife.

2. What street does Jane live on?

3. When does Carlos get up in the morning?

4. How does Suzi get to school?

What does Jimmy want for lunch?

⑤

Where does Lucy buy groceries?

⑥

What kind of music does Dallas like?

⑦

When does Milton have dinner?

⑧

When does Maria go to bed?

⑨

▶ **PAIR WORK** • *Ask each other the same questions.*

A: **Who do you talk to every day?**

B: **I talk to my sister.**

GRAMMAR • Simple Present Tense

Affirmative		
He She	walks	to school every day.

Negative		
He She	doesn't (does not)	take the bus.

Irregular verbs:
do - does
watch - watches
relax - relaxes

▶ **WRITING** • *Write affirmative and negative sentences about the people in the pictures. After you finish, read the sentences out loud.*

(1) Ellen Grayson (work) __works__ as a receptionist at an employment agency. (2) She (like) __doesn't like__ her job because it's boring. (3) She (do) _____ the same thing every day. (4) Ellen's problem is that she (have) _____ any fun. (5) She really (need) _____ a vacation.

It's Saturday afternoon. (1) Ernie is happy because he (work) _____ on Saturdays. (2) He (stay) _____ home and (watch) _____ TV all day. (3) Ernie's wife is upset with him because he (help) _____ her with the housework. (4) She (think) _____ Ernie is lazy.

(1) Jane Doe (live) _____ in a small house on Hill Street. (2) Her house (have) _____ a big yard, but it (have) _____ a nice porch. (3) Every day Jane (relax) _____ on the porch with her cats. (4) Jane (love) _____ cats, but she (like) _____ dogs very much.

▶ **DISCUSSION** • *Do these people remind you of anyone you know — a friend, a neighbor, or a member of your family? What do they have in common?*

Example: **"Ellen reminds me of my neighbor. He also works in an office, and he doesn't like his job."**

Yes/No Question			Short Answers						
Does	he she	work on Saturday?	Yes,	he she	does.	No,	he she	doesn't.	

▶ **PAIR WORK** • *Ask and answer questions.*

1. A: **Does Ellen like her job?**
   B: **No, she doesn't. She hates her job.**

2. A: **Does Mr. Wick need a secretary?**
   B: **Yes, he does.**

3. Does Amy study at the library after school?

4. Does Milton drive to work?

5. Does Ernie work on Saturdays?

6. Does Jane shop at discount stores?

7. Does Lulu drive a small car?

8. Does Carlos play the guitar?

9. Does Ken want a guitar?

GRAMMAR • Simple Present Tense

Where	do	they	live? work?

They	live work	in Hollywood.

▶ 🎧 *Listen. Listen and repeat.*

▶ **WRITING** • *Fill in the answers.*
Then read the conversations aloud.

▶ **PAIR WORK** • *Practice the conversations.*

1. **Where do Lisa and her friends hang out?**

   They hang out at the mall.

2. **Where do the boys play baseball?**

3. **Where do Jack and Jill study after school?**

4. **Where do Lucy and Grover shop?**

Where do these people work?

5

Where do Becky and Jimmy eat lunch?

6

Where do Ken and Suzi exercise?

7

Where do Carlos and Maria go dancing?

8

Where do people have picnics in the summer?

9

▶ **GROUP WORK** • *Ask each other where you hang out, eat lunch, study, exercise, shop.*
A: **Where do you hang out?** B: **I hang out at the Amazon Cafe. I go there with my friends.**

GRAMMAR • Simple Present Tense

Affirmative	Negative
They listen to classical music.	They don't like rock music.

▶ **WRITING** • *Write affirmative and negative sentences about Mr. and Mrs. Grand. After you finish, read the sentences out loud.*

1. (live in a big house) <u>They live in a big house.</u>

2. (worry about money) <u>They don't worry about money.</u>

3. (have a lot of employees) _____

4. (work in the garden) _____

5. (have a big car) _____

6. (take the bus) _____

7. (love fine food) _____

8. (like fast food) _____

9. (wear expensive clothes) _____

10. (shop at discount stores) _____

GRAMMAR • Simple Present Tense

Yes/No Question		
Do	they	get up early? walk to school?

Short Answers					
Yes,	they	do.	No,	they	don't.

▶ **PAIR WORK** • *Ask and answer questions.*

1. A: **Do Lucy and Grover shop at Junior's?**
   B: **Yes, they do.**

2. A: **Do Max and Louise work at the library?**
   B: **No, they don't. They work at the bank.**

3. Do Mr. and Mrs. Garcia live on Lime Street?

4. Do Joe and Eddie need money?

5. Do Mr. and Mrs. Grand have money problems?

6. Do the girls walk to school?

7. Do the boys play video games after school?

8. Do Daisy and Dallas enjoy country music?

9. Do Mr. and Mrs. Lee have an orange tree?

TOPIC • Music

🎧 MUSICAL STYLES • *Listen.*

classical   jazz

rock   country   rap

🎧 LISTENING TO MUSIC • *Check (✓) the musical styles you hear.*

1. ❏ classical ❏ jazz ❏ rock ❏ country ❏ rap
2. ❏ classical ❏ jazz ❏ rock ❏ country ❏ rap
3. ❏ classical ❏ jazz ❏ rock ❏ country ❏ rap
4. ❏ classical ❏ jazz ❏ rock ❏ country ❏ rap
5. ❏ classical ❏ jazz ❏ rock ❏ country ❏ rap

▶ DISCUSSION • *First answer the teacher; then form small groups and ask each other these questions.*

1. What kind of music do you like?
2. Is there any kind of music that you don't like?
3. What's your opinion of jazz?
4. What kind of music is popular in your country?
5. Who are your favorite singers and groups?
6. Do you like to sing? When? Where?
7. Do you play a musical instrument?
8. Where do you go to hear live music?

▶ 🎧 **MOVIES** • *Listen and repeat.*

comedies

dramas

adventure movies

science fiction movies

westerns

cartoons

▶ **DISCUSSION** • *Answer the teacher; then form small groups and ask each other these questions.*

- What kind of movies do you like?
- What's your favorite movie?
- Who's your favorite actor?

- Are there any good movies playing now?
- Who do you go to the movies with?
- Are there any movie theaters around here?

▶ 🎧 **TV PROGRAMS** • *Listen and repeat.*

comedies

dramas

news programs

sports programs

▶ **DISCUSSION** • *Answer the teacher; then form small groups and ask each other these questions.*

- When do you watch TV?
- How many hours a day do you watch TV?
- What kind of TV programs do you like?

- What's your favorite program?
- When is it on?
- Do you watch… (name of program)?

VOCABULARY

NOUNS

Music
classical
country
jazz
rap
rock

Movies
adventure
cartoon
comedy
drama
science fiction
western

Other
actor
appointment
cards
discount store
employee
group
member
movie theater
musical instrument
opinion
picnic
president
program
secretary
teeth
video game

VERBS
become
brush
do
exercise
find
hang out
hear
stay
worry

ADJECTIVES
lazy
popular

ADVERBS
early
fast
late
mostly

PREPOSITION
after
around

CONJUNCTION
because

EXPRESSIONS

Talking about routines

What time do you get up?
   I get up at…
When does he go to bed?
   He goes to bed at…

Talking about yourself

I get up early.
I don't sleep late.
I work fast.
I don't waste time.

Asking someone's opinion

What's your opinion?
   They look nice.

Asking about price

How much does it cost?
   Two thousand dollars.

Other

Oh, yeah.   Great!   I bet…
It's the same thing   Excellent!   I'm sure…

PRONUNCIATION

▶ **A** 🎧 *Listen and repeat. Notice the pronunciation of the **s** endings.*

/**s**/	/**z**/	/**iz**/
want**s**	live**s**	brush**es**
take**s**	play**s**	exercis**es**
keep**s**	stud**ies**	relax**es**

_____	<u>cleans</u>	_____
_____	_____	_____
_____	_____	_____
_____	_____	_____

▶ **B** 🎧 *Listen and write these verbs in the correct columns.*

cleans	looks	dances	opens	makes	goes
washes	gives	sleeps	closes	teaches	eats

▶ **C** 🎧 *What do these people do every day? Listen to the verb in each sentence.*

1. He <u>eats</u> an apple.

2. She _____ her teeth.

3. He _____ the newspaper.

4. She _____ the dishes.

5. He _____ the bus.

6. She _____ her car.

7. He _____ coffee.

8. He _____ TV.

9. She _____ the piano.

▶ **D** *Complete the sentences in Part C. Then read each sentence out loud.*

GRAMMAR SUMMARY

SIMPLE PRESENT Affirmative

He She	lives	
I You We They	live	in New York.

Negative

He She	doesn't (does not)	
I You We They	don't (do not)	live in New York.

Interrogative

Does	he she	
Do	I you we they	live in New York?

Short Answers

Yes,	he she	does.		No,	he she	doesn't.
	I you we they	do.			I you we they	don't.

Questions with WHO, WHAT, WHEN, WHERE

Who	lives in that house?	Mrs. Brown.
What	does your brother do?	He's a mechanic.
When	do you have lunch?	At one o'clock.
Where	do the girls study?	At the library.

CONTENTS

Chapter

CARTOON STORY

🎧 *It's Sunday afternoon and Jason is taking a walk in the park. Listen and practice.*

QUESTIONS

1. Who does Jason meet at the park?
2. Why does Lisa come to the park on weekends?
3. Is she enjoying the music today?
4. What does Lisa do?
5. Are her students lucky? Why?
6. Do you think Lisa likes Jason? Why?

STARTING A CONVERSATION

▶ 🎧 **WRITING** • *Amanda Standfast and Henry Bell are meeting for the first time. Listen to Amanda's questions and Henry's possible answers below each picture. Write the answer you like best or give your own answer to each question. After you finish, practice the conversation with a partner.*

- I don't think so.
- No, it's too cold.
- No, I hate this weather.
- Other.

- I come here once or twice a week.
- Yes, I come here every day.
- No, this is my first time.
- Other.

- It's okay.
- No, I think it's terrible.
- You call this music?
- Other.

- I'm a salesman.
- I'm looking for a job.
- It's none of your business.
- Other.

▶ **PAIR WORK** • *Start a conversation with the person next to you. Use some of Amanda's questions, and ask some original questions. In a good conversation, each speaker asks and answers questions.*

GRAMMAR REVIEW • Simple Present Tense

🎧 *Listen. Listen and repeat.*

▶ **PAIR WORK** • *Practice the conversations.*

▶ **WRITING** • *Fill in the questions and answers. Then read the conversations aloud.*

1. Ben and Sara / a dishwasher? | have

Do Ben and Sara have a dishwasher?

No, they don't.

2. Jean / blond hair? | have

Does Jean have blond hair?

Yes, she does.

3. Lucy and Grover / a fireplace? | have

4. Jason / a big car? | have

5. Mr. and Mrs. Doe / rock music? | like

6. Suzi / roses? | like

7. Becky and Jimmy / ice cream? | like

8. Mr. Ruffcorn / birds? | like

GRAMMAR REVIEW • Simple Present Tense

▶ 🎧 *Look at the pictures and listen to the conversations.*

▶ **WRITING** • *Begin the questions using* **What, Where, When, How, How often, What kind of.**

▶ **PAIR WORK** • *Practice the conversations.*

How often does Suzi exercise?

Three times a week.

①

_____ food do Bob and Alice like?

Mexican food.

②

_____ does Ken see his friends?

On the weekend.

③

_____ do Mr. and Mrs. Baker live?

On Rock Street.

④

5. _____ languages does Maria speak?

English and Spanish.

Good morning. Buenos días.

6. _____ does Carlos brush his teeth?

Twice a day.

7. _____ do your neighbors watch TV?

After dinner.

8. _____ work does Pam do?

She's a nurse.

9. _____ do Becky and Jimmy go to school?

They take the bus.

▶ **PAIR WORK** • *Ask each other the same questions.*

A: **How often do you exercise?**   B: **I exercise every day.**

BEAUTIFUL HOMES

▶ **CLASS ACTIVITY** • *Look at the different homes in the pictures. Which home is the most beautiful? The most modern? The most expensive? Which house is your favorite?*

1. a house in the city

2. a house by the sea

3. a log cabin in the mountains

4. a farm house in the country

▶ **WORK ALONE** • *The home in the pictures below has many nice features. Which features are important to you? Which features are not very important? Number the six features in their order of importance. Number one is the most important and number six is the least important.*

___ a porch ___ fruit trees ___ a garden ___ a balcony ___ a patio ___ a swimming pool

JANET'S DREAM HOUSE

▶ 🎧 *Listen to Janet talk about her dream house.*

My dream house is an old-fashioned house in the country. It has large windows because I like a house that is sunny and cheerful. In the living room, there's a fireplace, a piano, and a big, comfortable sofa. My dream house is ideal for a family of four. It has three bedrooms, and there's a bathroom next to each bedroom. Best of all, there's a swimming pool in the backyard. That's my favorite place in the summertime when the weather gets hot.

▶ **QUESTIONS**

1. Where is Janet's dream house?
2. How many bedrooms does it have?
3. What's in the living room?
4. Why does Janet's dream house have large windows?
5. Where is Janet's favorite place on hot, summer days?

▶ **DISCUSSION** • *What are some features that make a house special?*

▶ **WORD POWER** • *Here are some typical words we use to talk about our homes.*

big = large	quiet ≠ noisy
ideal = perfect	large ≠ small
quiet = peaceful	cheap ≠ expensive
new = modern	modern ≠ old-fashioned
cheerful = sunny	front yard ≠ back yard
cozy = small, comfortable and warm	hot, summer days ≠ cold, winter nights

▶ **COMPOSITION** • *Write a paragraph describing your dream house. For ideas, look at the pictures on these pages. Look at the vocabulary in WORD POWER, and Janet's description of her dream house. What do you like best about your dream house?*

LIFE SKILL • Locating Places

▶ 🎧 *Look and listen. Then read out loud.*

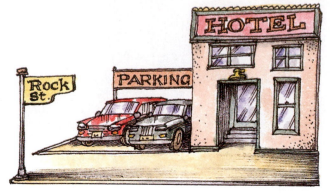

There's a parking lot on Rock Street,
next to the hotel.

There's a bakery on Central Avenue,
between the coffee shop and the bank.

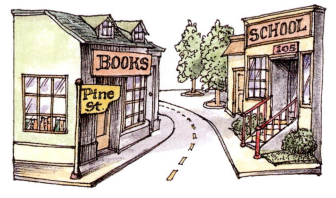

There's a bookstore on Pine Street,
across from the school.

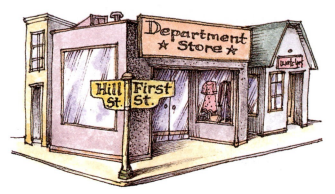

There's a department store on First Street,
on the corner of First and Hill.

▶ **PAIR WORK** • *Ask and answer questions. Use **between, next to, across from,** and **on the corner of** in your answers.*

1. barbershop?

A: **Excuse me. Is there a barbershop around here?**

B: **Yes. There's a barbershop on Main Street, between the flower shop and the hotel.**

2. gas station?

A: **Excuse me. Is there a gas station around here?**

B: **Yes. There's a gas station on Hill Street, on the corner of Hill and Lake.**

1. barbershop?

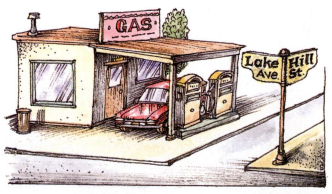

2. gas station?

3. bank?

4. movie theater?

5. supermarket?

6. laundromat?

7. hotel?

8. drugstore?

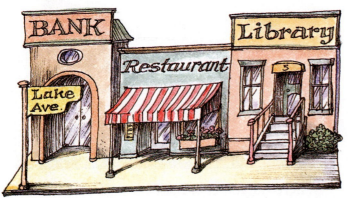

9. restaurant?

10. post office?

COMMUNITY RESOURCES

▶ 🎧 *Look and listen. Then answer the question below each picture.*

1. Jane is cashing a check at Union Bank on Lake Avenue.

Where do you keep your money?

2. Mr. and Mrs. Baker are buying groceries at Junior's Market on Hill Street.

Where do you buy groceries?

3. Jack and Jill are studying at the library on Central Avenue.

Where do you study?

4. Nick is getting a haircut at Clancy's Barbershop on First Street.

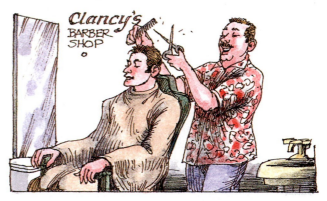

Where do you go for a haircut?

5. Suzi is mailing some letters at the post office on Main Street.

Where do you go to mail letters?

6. Carlos and Maria are exercising at Spike's Gym on Franklin Avenue.

Where do you exercise?

7. Becky and Jimmy are having lunch at the school cafeteria.

Where do you have lunch?

8. Donna is shopping for clothes at the Bargain Shop on First Street.

Where do you shop for clothes?

9. Bruno is washing his clothes at the laundromat on Dixon Avenue.

Where do you wash your clothes?

10. Daisy and Dallas are dancing at the Cowboy Saloon on Mason Street.

Where do you go dancing?

▶ **PAIR WORK** • *Ask and answer questions.*

go to the library

A: **How often do you go to the library?**

B: **I go to the library once a week.**

   OR   **I go about three times a week.**

   OR   **I go to the library every day.**

   OR   **I never go to the library.**

1. read the newspaper
2. buy groceries
3. brush your teeth
4. exercise
5. get a haircut
6. take the bus
7. go downtown
8. shop for clothes
9. see your friends
10. go dancing

Frequency Expressions
every day
every week
every weekend
once a day/week/month
twice a day/week/month
three times a day/week/month
never

TOPIC • Health Problems

▶ **HEALTH PROBLEMS** • *Listen and repeat.*

1. a headache

2. a toothache

3. red eyes

4. a cold

5. a stomachache

6. chest pain

7. a sore throat

8. insomnia

▶ **PAIR WORK** • *Ask and answer questions about the health problems of these people.*

1. Grover

A: **Why is Grover taking aspirin?**

B: **He's taking aspirin because he has a headache.**

1. Why is Grover taking aspirin?

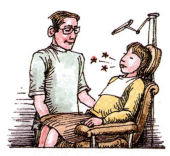

2. Why is Becky seeing the dentist?

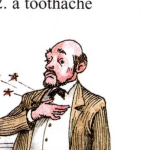

3. Why is Jane using eye drops?

4. Why is Carlos taking vitamin C?

5. Why is Mabel taking antacid?

6. Why is Mr. Grand seeing the doctor?

7. Why is Suzi taking cough syrup?

8. Why is Ben drinking warm milk?

TOPIC • Health Remedies

▶ 🎧 *Listen. Listen and practice.*

A: Excuse me. Where is the antacid?

B: It's in aisle 5.

A: Thank you.

B: You're welcome.

▶ **PAIR WORK** • *Have similar conversations about these items:* (a) aspirin
(b) cough syrup (c) mouthwash (d) eye drops (e) cold medicine (f) toothbrushes

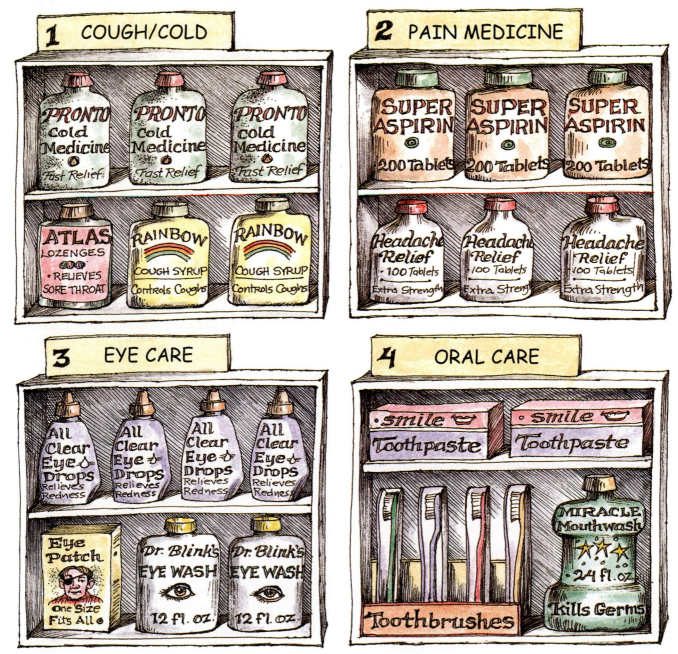

GRAND EXPECTATIONS

▶ 🎧 **PERSONAL INFORMATION** • *Read the profiles of Wendy and Fred.*

Name: _Wendy Walker_   Age: _28_
Occupation: _Police Officer_
Interests: _reading, listening to music, hiking, swimming, playing tennis_

▶ 🎧 *About me.*

I am a happy, outgoing, energetic person who is a lot of fun. I enjoy life, people, good food and music. I am lucky to have a wonderful family and close friends. I live in the Los Angeles area. I love Southern California for its great weather, beautiful mountains and sandy beaches. I like to be outdoors as much as possible. I enjoy hiking, playing tennis and swimming. I'm adventurous, and I like to try new things.

▶ **QUESTIONS**

1. Where does Wendy live?
2. What does she enjoy doing?
3. Do you think Wendy is an interesting person? Why or why not?
4. Do you know any women like Wendy?

Name: _Fred Fargo_   Age: _30_
Occupation: _Salesperson_
Interests: _birds, cartoons, video games, playing cards, having fun_

▶ 🎧 *About me.*

I am a very interesting person. I have brown hair and brown eyes, and I have a nice smile. I'm a little shy, but everybody says I'm a cool guy. I'm really fun to be with. I like to stay home and play video games or watch TV. I also enjoy relaxing. Sometimes I go to the park and feed the birds. I give them bread crumbs. It's a blast to feed the birds, and it doesn't cost much. I think the best things in life are cheap.

▶ **QUESTIONS**

1. What does Fred like to do?
2. Do you think Fred is an interesting person? Why or why not?
3. Do you think the best things in life are cheap, expensive or free?

▶ **WRITING** • *Imagine you are a member of Grand Expectations. Complete the profile with information about yourself.*

```
┌─────────────────────────────────┐
│                                 │
│                                 │
│                                 │
│           Your Photo            │
│                                 │
│                                 │
│                                 │
└─────────────────────────────────┘
```

Name: _____ Age: _____

Occupation: _____

Interests: _____

_____

▶ **PAIR WORK** • *Talk with your partner about your interests. Ask each other questions to get more information.*

▶ **COMPOSITION** • *Write a paragraph describing yourself. Use the description of Wendy Walker or Fred Fargo on page 156 as a model.*

About me.

_____

_____

_____

_____

_____

_____

_____

_____

_____

_____

▶ **PAIR WORK** • *Read your partner's personal description and ask questions to get more information. Tell the class the most interesting thing you learned about your partner.*

VOCABULARY

NOUNS

Health problems
cold
cough
headache
insomnia
red eyes
sore throat
stomachache
toothache

Health remedies
antacid
aspirin
cold medicine
cough syrup
eye drops
eye wash
lozenges
mouthwash

Other
area
balcony
comb
dentist
dishwasher
dream
entertainment
farmhouse
feature

haircut
log cabin
nurse
parking lot
patio
swimming pool
teeth
third grade
vitamin

VERBS
hate
feed
keep
mail
say
teach

ADJECTIVES
adventurous
cheerful
close
cozy
different
energetic
fortunate

ideal
modern
old-fashioned
outgoing
peaceful
sunny

SUPERLATIVE
most expensive ≠ least expensive
most important ≠ least important

ADVERB
sometimes

EXPRESSIONS

Asking for and giving locations
Is there a bank around here?
Yes. There's one next to the hotel.
        …across from the park.

Talking about the weather
Beautiful day, isn't it?
   It's lovely.
In the summertime, when
the weather gets hot…

Giving opinions
It's okay.
It's a blast.
I think it's terrible.
I don't think so.

Talking about where people live
They live in the city.
    …by the sea.
    …in the mountains.
    …in the country.

Talking about routines
How often do you…?
    …every day.
    …every week.
    …every weekend.
    …once a day/week.
    …twice a day/week.
    …three times a day/week.

Talking about activities
I enjoy hiking.
    …swimming.
She likes to sing.
    …dance.

Asking permission
Is it okay if I sit here?

Other
This is my first time.
Me, too.

It doesn't cost much.
It's none of your business.

Are you serious?
I really mean it.

PRONUNCIATION

A 🎧 *Listen and repeat. Notice the two pronunciations of* **th.**

/θ/		/ð/	
<u>th</u>ink	ba<u>th</u>	<u>th</u>en	fa<u>th</u>er
<u>th</u>ank	mou<u>th</u>	<u>th</u>at	mo<u>th</u>er
<u>th</u>irsty	heal<u>th</u>	<u>th</u>ere	toge<u>th</u>er

B 🎧 **DICTATION** • *Listen and complete the sentences.*

1. We study <u>together</u> on <u>Thursdays</u>.

2. I _____ my _____ is beautiful.

3. _____ you for _____ lovely flowers.

4. I get _____ when the _____ is hot.

5. My _____ is in good _____.

6. _____ are _____ rooms in ___ hotel.

7. My _____ is taking a _____.

8. Your _____ are over _____.

9. Be careful _____ _____ _____!

C **PAIR WORK** • *Take turns saying the sentences in Part B.*

TEST

May I use the phone?

I'm looking for the tomatoes.

They're _____.

1. a. Very good.   c. It's working.
   b. Yes, of course.   d. That's for sure.

2. a. delicious   c. over there
   b. expensive   d. right here

3. The boys _____ football now.

   a. plays   c. is playing
   b. playing   d. are playing

4. Sara is busy. She _____.

   a. is studying   c. study
   b. are studying   d. studies

5. Grover _____ Mexican food.

   a. love   c. loving
   b. loves   d. do love

6. Some people _____ every day.

   a. exercise   c. does exercise
   b. exercises   d. is exercising

7. Ellen _____ her job.

   a. no like   c. doesn't like
   b. don't like   d. likes not

8. Mr. Denby is unhappy when his students _____ their homework.

   a. do not   c. don't do
   b. not do   d. doesn't do

9. "Are Bob and Alice working today?"
   "_____."

   a. Yes, they are.
   b. No, they aren't.
   c. Yes, they do.
   d. No, they don't.

10. "Does Lulu like her new car?"
    "_____."

    a. Yes, she is.
    b. Yes, she do.
    c. Yes, she likes.
    d. Yes, she does.

TEST

11. a. This   c. These
    b. That   d. Those

12. a. this   c. these
    b. that   d. those

13. Oranges are my favorite _____.

    a. color   c. fruit
    b. vegetable   d. drink

14. We eat a big _____ every morning.

    a. food   c. lunch
    b. breakfast   d. dinner

15. "What do you do?"
    "_____"

    a. I'm busy.
    b. I'm fine, thank you.
    c. I'm doing my homework.
    d. I'm a mechanic.

16. "Is it okay if I use your computer?"
    "_____"

    a. Sure.
    b. You're welcome.
    c. Come on.
    d. That's right.

17. "_____ does Mike like his job?"
    "Because it's interesting."

    a. How   c. Why
    b. How much   d. When

18. "_____ do you exercise?"
    "Three times a week."

    a. How many   c. When
    b. How often   d. Where

19. a. wash   c. take
    b. buy   d. forget

20. a. hear   c. take
    b. answer   d. hold

TEST

_____ name is Zola.

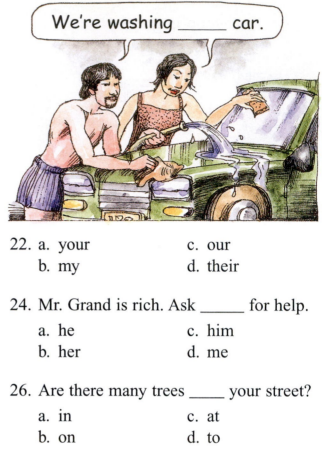

We're washing _____ car.

21. a. Your   c. His
    b. My   d. Her

22. a. your   c. our
    b. my   d. their

23. I'm your friend. Listen to _____.
    a. I   c. you
    b. me   d. him

24. Mr. Grand is rich. Ask _____ for help.
    a. he   c. him
    b. her   d. me

25. We live ____ the city.
    a. in   c. at
    b. on   d. to

26. Are there many trees ____ your street?
    a. in   c. at
    b. on   d. to

27. _____ some apples on the table.
    a. It has   c. There is
    b. They're   d. There are

28. We don't have _____ bread.
    a. a   c. no
    b. any   d. some

Is there any soup in the pot?

Are there any cookies in the jar?

29. a. Yes, there is.
    b. No, there isn't.
    c. Yes, there are.
    d. No, there aren't.

30. a. Yes, there is.
    b. No, there isn't.
    c. Yes, there are.
    d. No, there aren't.